"This charming book is a simple, effective reminder of how to present truth, and it carries with it a fair amount of wisdom about finding truth in the first place. Professor Topping has produced a guide accessible and useful to those of all ages and experience levels, in the classroom, the political setting, and the pulpit. It will prove doubly edifying, first for those who read it, then for those who listen to those who read it. May both groups be large in number!"
—JOSEPH R. WOOD, Institute of World Politics

"This is a splendid introduction to what you need to know to communicate wisely and well. It is clearly written with engaging examples that demonstrate the practical relevance of age-old principles to today's communication. Read, learn, and enjoy this book. Then recommend it to friends."
—QUENTIN SCHULTZE, Arthur H. DeKruyter Chair in Faith and Communication, Calvin College, author of *An Essential Guide to Public Speaking* and *Habits of the High-Tech Heart*

"*The Elements of Rhetoric* is that rarest of rhetorical treats: a playfully serious and seriously playful *summa* of the art of communication—classical education at its very best!"
—RAYMOND F. HAIN, Assistant Professor of Philosophy, Providence College

"Leading by example, Ryan Topping delivers a handy guide for all of us who rely on the art of persuasion. *The Elements of Rhetoric* is a gem."
—DANIEL B. COUPLAND, Associate Professor of Education, Hillsdale College, co-author of *Well-Ordered Language: The Curious Child's Guide to Grammar*

"This is the book I have sought for 35 years. As a trial lawyer, partner, elected official, board member, editor, fund-raiser, author, and lecturer, I am called on every few days to give closing arguments, formal remarks, speeches, sales pitches, and presentations. For those like me, for whom public speaking and writing is their stock-in-trade, this book is a must-have daily companion."

—MICHAEL C. GILLERAN, Business & IP Trial Lawyer & Partner, Burns & Levinson, LLP, Boston, MA; author of *Massachusetts Practice: The Law of Chapter 93A*

"Witty, vivid, and clear, *The Elements of Rhetoric* is bound to capture the minds and hearts of students in high school and across college campuses. Ryan Topping presents the classical Greek terms of logic and persuasion in a memorable way, illustrating them with passages and advice from authors who span the spectrum of time and place: from Homer and Caesar to Koestler and Rowling. *Elements* will empower students to engage audiences of diverse backgrounds by enhancing the appeal and approach of their debates, public speaking, and written arguments. This versatile guide can supplement course material from any discipline in order to help students polish presentations and essays."

—ANN MARIE KLEIN, Department of Catholic Studies, University of St. Thomas, MN

The Elements of Rhetoric

THE
ELEMENTS
OF
Rhetoric

*How to Write and Speak
Clearly and Persuasively*

A GUIDE FOR STUDENTS,
TEACHERS, POLITICIANS & PREACHERS

by
Ryan N.S. Topping

 Angelico Press

First published
in the USA by Angelico Press
© Ryan N.S. Topping 2016

For information, address:
Angelico Press
4709 Briar Knoll Dr.
Kettering, OH 45429
info@angelicopress.com

978-1-62138-196-9 pb
978-1-62138-197-6 ebook

Cover Design: Michael Schrauzer
Cover image: Frontispiece of Quintilian's *Instituto oratoria*,
ed. by Pieter Burman(n) the Elder, Leiden 1720

CONTENTS

Introduction

IMAGINE this scenario. You have a baby. You pinch for a down payment. You spot your dream home—or what you thought would be. The kitchen looks great, but the property is on the corner of "Brown" and "*Kings* Crescent." Huh? If the gals at City Hall can't spell, are you going to trust them with your taxes? As was recently reported, Birmingham's (not Birminghams) City Council has now banned apostrophes, and the township of Mid-Devon in the southwest corner of England nearly did the same. The township's proposed legislation declared that streets should not be given names "that may be considered or construed as obscene or racist," and further: "In order to avoid causing offence either by inclusion or exclusion, no street shall be named after any living person." And then: "All punctuation, including apostrophes, shall be avoided." After banning local heroes, I suppose English punctuation comes next on the list.

It takes a certain kind of *panache* to legislate that your town cannot publicly honor the great men and women who live there, especially when your town has produced the likes of the sea-explorer and vanquisher of the Spanish Armada, Sir Francis Drake; the poet Samuel Coleridge; and murder mystery empress Agatha Christie. But who needs murder mysteries when the local kids cant [sic] read them anyway?

Don't let anyone tell you news is always bad. Here was one instance where common sense prevailed. Sadly, Birmingham's ban remained; but only days after the council made its bid to rid confusion, the locals in Devon came out for a fight. *The Telegraph* reported the decision was to be reversed. Officials said punctuation could stay.[1] Thanks, Big Brother!

---

[1] "Apostrophe Ban Takes U-Turn," *The Telegraph*, March 19, 2013.

Language is always on the move. What passed for good grammar, for elegant speech, for a persuasive style in the days of Will Shakespeare might not directly move readers in the era of Dan Brown. Still, most rules abide. We ignore them to our peril. As with a change in the Constitution, inflict a move too quickly and a lot of innocent heads will be lost.

G.K. Chesterton once remarked that while the aim of the sculptor is to convince us that he is a sculptor, the aim of the orator is "to convince us that he is not an orator." In this case what is true of the preacher is true for the politician, the professor, and his students. In fact, it holds for anyone who needs to make his case convincing.

As classically conceived, the chief aim of rhetoric is to arm the good against the assaults of the bad. Truth, of course, retains a native appeal. Yet truth unadorned is usually truth ignored. Follow these 26 rules and you'll learn how to show Lady Philosophy at her best.

R.N.S. Topping
Thomas More College, NH

I

Logos:
Rational Speech

Master grammar—observe three precepts—
Learn a little logic—Avoid fallacies

1. Master grammar

Logos, *pathos*, and *ethos* are the three means open to you to influence your listener. As teaching is your primary aim, clarity is your first obligation. *Logos* means, quite simply, articulate speech. Clarity is your first duty because without it the listener cannot even offer you that most elementary of courtesies, the honor of disagreement.

> "Who did you pass on the road?" the King went on, holding his hand out to the messenger for some hay.
> "Nobody," said the messenger.
> "Quite right," said the King; "this young lady saw him too. So of course Nobody walks slower than you."
> "I do my best," the Messenger said in a sulky tone. "I'm sure nobody walks much faster than I do!"
> "He can't do that," said the King, "or else he'd have been here first..."[1]

The messenger intended "nobody" to mean *no person*, while the King took "nobody" to refer to *a proper name*. Alice's conversations delight because the characters take everything literally. You only catch the joke, though, if you see the difference between the univocal and equivocal use of words. Even nonsense depends upon good sense.

---

[1] Lewis Carroll, *Through the Looking-Glass and What Alice Found There* (Mineola, NY: Dover Publications, 1999), 66–67.

As the adventures of Alice illustrate, if nobody learns the rules it's hard for anybody to keep them. Apparently, employers' number one complaint about new hires these days is that they cannot read.[2] It's a pity, not only because of garbled office memos; I say, let the children master grammar so that they can enjoy Lewis Carroll!

Brace yourself. It's hard being a stickler for syntax and basic punctuation. Advertisers work against you. Text-messengers think you uptight. And each time you've breezed down a grocery aisle that announced "potato's ½ price," or heard people speak of "data," "phenomena," and "media" as though they referred to single subjects, you've seen the mischievous work of miscreant advertisers. "But," the critic retorts, "so long as we understand each other, why bother with the niceties?" Why bother, indeed?

Disrespect grammar and, in the first instance, you lose credibility. I'm not sure how many months this restaurant in Florida has been in business, but my guess is that it won't survive long. Here is a sign posted outside one of their restrooms.

Employee's
Must wash there hands
Before returning to work!

Credibility is one thing. Sense is another. With only a few strokes a little punctuation can make a big difference:

No cats are mean!
No, cats are mean.

A woman, without her man, is nothing.
A woman: without her, man is nothing.

---

[2] Tom Bradshaw and Bonnie Nichols, "Reading at Risk: A Survey of Literary Reading in America—Report #46" (Washington, DC: National Endowment for the Arts, 2004).

Reasonable speech begins with right grammar. Irony, equivocation, puns, and much of the fun of language depend, oddly enough, upon a rather strict grasp of a few stodgy conventions.

2. Observe three precepts

If you are starting out in your scholastic or professional career, you may wish to consider getting to know Strunk and White's classic *The Elements of Style*. After you've worked through that text, set upon your desk the following three principles of style. Observe them.

Precept 1: Omit needless words.

Nearly anything you write can be improved. When preparing an essay or a speech expect to compose at least three drafts. Each time you comb through your text omit words that either are unnecessary or could be replaced by a word that is more precise. Here are common phrases that can be reduced:

She is a lady who…	She
Owing to the fact that…	Since
In spite of the fact that…	Although
There is no question that…	Certainly
No minors will be able to…	No minors can
That man, who is his father, likes…	His father likes

Fewer words are not always better words. The reader's or listener's patience, however, should not be put to the test. A paragraph is like a finely tuned bicycle. Words, phases, and sentences should each work to contribute to your end. Omit superfluous parts.

Precept 2: Use the active voice.

The passive voice works well when anonymity is desired. For many years my mother-in-law was a librarian. She knew how to give orders, like this one:

> *It has been decided* that no minors will *be able to rent* videos at this library without parental approval.

Here the lack of a specific agent (who decided this rule?) and the roundabout description ("be able to rent") add to the librarian's fiat a sense of objectivity and authority. Outside of the requirements for signage and commands, however, the active voice is normally the one to be preferred.

Young writers in particular are tempted to claim a feigned objectivity. I cannot say how many papers I have read which begin like this:

> In this essay the political effects of the French Revolution upon the English aristocracy *will be discussed.*

Some academic disciplines train their students to become proficient in the art of the government memo. So be it. Unless convention dictates otherwise, in nearly every case it is better to claim the essay as your own. Try instead:

> In this essay I discuss the political effects of the French Revolution upon the English aristocracy.

A last problem with the passive voice is that it often requires more, that is to say needless, words.

He was hit by the ball…	The ball hit him
The red oak was made extinct…	The red oak vanished
She was awakened by the birds…	The birds woke her

Precept 3: Use parallel structure.
Express similar ideas in a similar form. This is one of the language's most pleasing devices. Likeness of structure helps the

reader or listener to grasp quickly the connection between related ideas. Buddha offered this advice that is not only sage but memorable:

> All that we are is defined by our thoughts: it begins
> where our thoughts begin, it moves where our thoughts
> move, and it rests where our thoughts rest.

Here is a good example from the Book of Ecclesiastes:

> For everything there is a season, and a time for every
>   matter under heaven:
> a time to be born, and a time to die;
> a time to plant, and a time to pluck up what is planted;
> a time to kill, and a time to heal;
> a time to break down, and a time to build up…

Especially when making lists, decide upon a form and stick to it. Correlative expressions (both, and; either, or; first, second; on the one hand, on the other hand) should follow a predictable pattern. Here is Beatrix Potter's skillful description of a naughty bunny.[3]

> First he ate some lettuces and some French beans; and
> then he ate some radishes; and then, feeling rather sick,
> he went to look for some parsley.

Below is a melancholic recommendation to architects living during a period of economic prosperity but cultural decline:

> The age of invention is gone by, and that of criticism has
> succeeded: it remains for us, if we cannot rival the beau-

---

[3] From *The Tale of Peter Rabbit*, in *Selected Tales from Beatrix Potter* (London: Frederick Warne, 2007), 13–14.

ties of our predecessors, to avoid their defects; to apply
with judgment, if we cannot invent with genius; and to
follow the guidance of just system, if we cannot track the
flights of imagination.[3]

Finally, here is a good rendering of Julius Caesar's marvelous
opening to *The Gallic War*, followed by what he might have written if he hadn't been Julius Caesar. Note the differences in structure:

The whole of Gaul is divided
into three parts, one of which
the Belgae inhabit, the
Aquitani another, and the third
a people who in their own language are called "Celts," but in
ours, "Gauls." They all differ
among themselves in respect of
language, way of life, and
laws.[4]

The whole of Gaul is divided
into three parts. One of these
the Belgae inhabit. The
Aquitani inhabit another part.
Another part is inhabited by a
people who in their own language are called "Celts," but in
ours, "Gauls." They all differ
among themselves in respect of
language; they also differ in
their way of life, and again in
their laws.

3. Learn a little logic

Now for the fun stuff. Whereas grammar governs conventions
for clear speech among men, logic is the language of God. Up
until the Second World War nearly anyone who passed through a
European or American university would have taken a basic
course in logic structured around what is known as "the three
acts of the mind." One reason why a grasp of the three acts is

---

[3] John Betjeman, *Ghastly Good Taste* (London: Century, 1986), 4.
[4] Julius Caesar, *The Gallic War*, translation by Carolyn Hammond (Oxford: Oxford University Press, 2008), 3.

useful is that it can help you spot the mistake that lies behind the most common logical fallacies.

The three acts refer to the three kinds of mental activity: understanding, judging, and reasoning. Each act works upon a different kind of object: terms, propositions, and syllogisms, respectively. Thinking upon those objects yields, in each case, one of two outcomes. Thus: a term can be either known or unknown; a proposition may either be true or false; a syllogism, valid or invalid.

The mind, like any other tool, can be used well or badly. Learn to use it well. Whether we like it or not, and whether we can name the rules or not, logic governs how the mind grasps truth. It's wired into us. Evidently, it is also programmed into the fabric of the universe.

Suppose you meet a friend who doubts the laws of logic. Ask them: by what faculty? Better, invite them to consider the next time they go to redeem their Super-Faithful-Flyer points for a free far-off get-away: why do I think it acceptable to fling my body 40,000 feet into the sky? Well, that's easy. Each time they step onto an airplane, they illustrate their faith in fairy dust.

Yes, that's all it is. We've built planes that float in the air because we've learned a little about the magic that binds physics to mathematics. No logic, no math; no math, no physics; no physics, no flight. Here in schematic form you see the basic building blocks of rational thinking.

Act of the Mind	Type of Object	Outcome
Understanding	Terms	Known/Unknown
The grasp of an essence, e.g.,		
'rational animal'	'Man'	
'three-sided figure'	'Triangle'	
Judging	Propositions	The True/The False
The evaluation of the truth of a proposition	"The man is red." "That dog is alive."	

Reasoning	Syllogisms	Valid/Invalid
The acquisition of new knowledge from old.	*"All men are mortal. Socrates is a man. Therefore, Socrates is mortal."*	

Before we turn to the mind's mistakes, let's fill in this sketch a bit. We can move through each act in turn.

By *understanding*, logicians refer to the mind's grasp of an essence or form. *Form* is an old word, but one worth remembering. Imagine two planks of oak cut from the same tree. A carpenter leaves behind one slab of wood and begins to work on another. An hour later the second plank has become a table. What changed? In their chemistry the two slabs remain identical. That is to say, in their matter, nothing changed: from the point of view of chemistry the two things remain one thing. And yet that is only from one rather limited point of view. From every other point of view, what altered is the wood's shape or *form*. The names we give to things identify these differences between things. Hence, to name the form is to mark the essence or essential shape of a given thing. "Table," "triangle," and "man" are each terms that name the form. The mind either succeeds or fails at grasping the forms behind the names.

We can take one more step. Definitions of terms are best when they are neither too broad nor too narrow. For example, "Man is a rational animal" remains sturdy because it hits the mean. To call men merely "rational" would leave out the body. To call men "animals" would forget the mind. Since we see both, a good definition will include both.

But, you ask, what if someone gave the wrong name? True, mistakes happen all the time. Hiking out in the woods we want to know whether the creature that has just crossed the trail in front of us is a "wolf" or a "Siberian Husky." What one man calls "murder" another claims is "self-defense." Such legitimate and frequently encountered difficulties show not the obtuseness of philosophy and science but why we can't live without them.

When natures cannot be immediately grasped we must rely upon the second act of the mind, what logicians call the act of judgment.

Judging refers to the evaluation of the truth or falsity of a proposition. Experimentation can help form your judgments, as can the advice of others. So if you're in the woods with an experienced hunter, you're in luck. He tells you: "That animal is a dog." Such a judgment is delivered in the form of a proposition—a statement with a subject and a predicate. In the example "Man is a rational animal," "Man" is the subject (the thing), while "rational animal" stands as the predicate (the description of the thing). The *subject* denotes what you wish to speak about; the *predicate* qualifies or adds to it.

Finally, there is *reasoning*. What could be more natural? Indeed, nothing could be more natural—nothing, that is, until someone disagrees with you! The frequency, variety, and intensity of intellectual disagreements give some indication of the importance of clear thinking about the nature of arguing. From thinking about things to judging affirmations about things, the mind can turn next to infer the connection *between* things. In the act of reasoning the mind posits causal links between terms and objects. In this third act of the mind, we move beyond mere observation and verbal clarification to science.

The syllogism is the motor behind every science. Insight is required, to be sure; but it is only through drawing the correct inference that we add to our knowledge. Consider the following statements.

P1 All men are mortal.	Every A is B
P2 Socrates is a man.	Some C is A
∴ Socrates is mortal.	∴ Some C is B

Constructing a syllogism is like constructing a house. You need at least two walls before you can erect another level. The walls are the premises. To build a second story, to build on top of these sturdy walls, you have to assume the foundations of the first story are sound. In the above example, the first two statements are *premises* and serve as the "walls" holding up your conclusion. The third statement, the *conclusion*, is the new second-story "floor" you hope to add. To argue convincingly you must move from known truths to some hitherto unknown or unobserved truth. Thus, when arguing, you ought to use premises that your listener will find compelling. Otherwise, if they reject your premises, they will disregard your conclusion. If you cannot find common ground on the lower levels, you'll never get to enjoy the views from the top floor together.

Take the following examples. Imagine a new principal arrives at your local high school and decides to prohibit students from listening to rap music while on school property. A group of students is angry. One student might conceivably reply with an argument along the following lines:

Every teen has the right to listen to rap music.	Every A is B
Every student at this school is a teen.	Every C is A
Every student at this school has the right to listen to rap music.	Every C is B

The argument is formally valid. But is the conclusion true? To find that out, at the least, both parties would have to explore the truth of the premises.

Now imagine you've just arrived at college. You're ready to encounter the wide world of debate. You overhear a discussion, after class, over whether abortion should be a legal right. One student offers the following syllogism:

Every child deserves the protections of law.	Every A is B
Every fetus is a child.	Every C is A
Every fetus deserves the protection of the law.	Every C is B

Having just come from Philosophy 101, you know how to identify this argument (logicians name the form of this argument a "Barbara"), and recognize it as formally valid, but see that this person's debating partner, who is pro-choice, stays unconvinced. How come?

This leads to the second important distinction, between truth and validity. *Truth* is the correspondence between mind and reality and applies to propositions. *Validity* refers to the formal relationship between propositions. In the above case, if the premises are both true, then as a matter of logical necessity so will be the conclusion. How, then, can rational minds disagree? If the pro-choicer is clever, he will also see that the syllogism is valid. Where he is likely to disagree is with the second premise ("Every fetus is a child").

I offer this piece of advice. When you arrive at an impasse, here is what you should not do. Do not simply recycle the same syllogism, tumbling it over and over like some shrinking shirt in a dryer: "Every child deserves the protections of law! ... Every fetus. ..." Move on. Find the disputed premises; ask questions of each other, and engage. If the fetus is not a human child, what is it?

The notion of the "three acts" goes back to Aristotle. By the Middle Ages it became a stock technique for training young minds to think. Whether you are thinking or speaking about constitutional law, or economics, or the life cycle of hawks, offend logic and eventually you will lose your listener.

4. Avoid six fallacies

The word *fallacy* comes from the Latin *fallo*, to fall or to deceive. A fallacy is an argument that appears to be valid but is not. Now that we've seen something of how the mind functions when it's firing on all cylinders, let's see what can go wrong under the hood.

There is no exhaustive list of mental mistakes. Aristotle named thirteen, and one modern logician has cataloged one-hundred and twelve. We'll take the top six, showing how each is a defect of one or another of the three acts.

Fallacies of Understanding: Amphiboly and Equivocation
An amphiboly is when an entire phrase has more than one plausible meaning. How would you feel about reading this, for instance?

> The manager reserves the right to exclude any man or
> woman they consider proper.

You're not sure whether to open or close the top button of your shirt. Being hustled out of your favorite restaurant is bad. The consequence of vague language in politics can be even worse. Do you remember the last round of election speeches you heard? Many politicians have been serving up rather thin broth for a few election cycles already. When politicians and journalists preach about their desire to bring "hope," to defend "rights," to protect "freedom," and to ensure "equality," do you know what they are talking about? Do you think they know what they are talking about? To *equivocate* is to conceal that you have used the same word first in one sense and then in another.

Words without definitions are like balloons without air. You can twirl them into any shape. It is instructive to recall that at the same moment the GUGB (forerunner to the KGB) was jailing priests and liquidating dissidents (some of my relatives were among the thousands who eventually fled), Stalin's 1936 *Constitution of the Soviet Union* defended both "freedom of conscience" in religion (article 124) and "freedom of speech" in the press (article 125). For the rhetorician, as for the logician, the first rule of clear speaking is that you define your terms—unless you have reason not to.

When the Fathers of the American Revolution gathered, the colonies were a series of loose allies who shared a grievance but as yet no common political identity. If the British could divide they would have surely conquered. Benjamin Franklin made this point admirably; at the signing of the Declaration of Independence on July 4, 1776 he employed this equivocation:

> We must all hang together, or assuredly we will all hang separately.

Here *hang* (like the term *nobody* earlier) is used twice in two different senses, and for that reason to memorable effect.

Examples from literature and everyday speech abound. Shakespeare is famous for his puns. In the opening to *Richard III*, "son" serves double duty by means of a trick on the ear:

> Now is the winter of our discontent
> Made glorious summer by this son of York;
> And all the clouds that low'r'd upon our house
> In the deep bosom of the ocean buried.

It's the sort of thing that gets Christmas parties off the ground and opens wedding speeches:

> What do you call Santa's helpers?
> Subordinate Clauses!

> You'll be happy to discover that my nephew is like a
>   horse.
> He's a stable animal.

The number of objects in the world may be infinite, but the number of words is not. According to the *Global Language Monitor*, just over 1 million English words are on the books (with one new word being added every 98 minutes). As the philosopher Martin Heidegger might have said after a few martinis, that's a lot of fish swimming in the sea of language.

Alas, few survive. The 20-volume *Oxford English Dictionary* lists 171,476 active words. And, by one estimate, the 100 most frequently used account for half of the terms in books. My point is this: language is limited, the cosmos is vast. This is one reason why words often carry multiple meanings. To avoid equivocation, define your terms.

Fallacies of Judging: *False Cause and* Post hoc ergo propter hoc
These two fallacies are close cousins. An error of judgment is a mistake not about terms but about *natures*. It is easy to assume connections between things, even when no connection exists. Any time we presume without justification that x caused y, we commit the fallacy of false cause.

The most common variety of the "false cause" is the *Post hoc ergo propter hoc* variety. *Post hoc ergo propter hoc* translates to "after this therefore on account of this." Here the mistake is to mistake temporal proximity for causal connection. Sometimes it is easy to spot:

The cock crows, the sun rises.
Therefore the cock causes the sun to rise.

The error in this judgment is to mistake correlation for causation. It is in fact true that cocks sing before sunrise. Birds may rouse us. Yet the sun, one suspects, pays little attention.

Other times the mistake is trickier to see. It is quite often assumed, for instance, that if the federal government offered more money to schools, public education in America would improve. One recent poll found that American adults say that inadequate funding is a top problem facing the schools in their communities. The connection seems clear. More money would lead to better salaries, and then to better teachers, and finally to better kids. Shouldn't educational inputs (cash, computers) lead to educational outcomes (grades, graduations)? Apparently, they do not.

Each year taxpayers spend about $12,500 per public-school student. This is an increase of more than 50% in real dollars over the last twenty-some years. And yet it's not clear that students seem to notice. The number of illiterate 17-year-olds is the same today as it was some twenty-five years ago (about 13%). On a recent standardized science test, 15-year-old Americans ranked 23rd. Hungary, Poland and Estonia ranked higher, each without spending as much as America on their public schools.[5]

When it comes to success in education, money matters. But so does culture, the health of the family, and the discipline of the child. Everyone acknowledges that public education in America needs repair. Next time you hear someone say more money alone will fix it you might whisper quietly to yourself, "False cause."

Fallacies of Reasoning: Ad Hominem and Ad Populum

When we make a mistake of reasoning, we fail accurately to connect premises with conclusions. The most frequent instance of this in private speech is the *Ad hominem* (against the man); the most frequent mistake of this sort in the press is, understandably, the *Ad populum* (appeal to the people).

Here's the difference. You have stepped into a discussion between two students over theories in biology. Debate has become heated. The senior, in frustration, finally tells the freshman student, "But you're a Mormon; therefore, what can you know about science?" Congratulations! As the conclusion doesn't follow, you will have just witnessed at college your first *ad hominem*. Then, imagine that same senior continues the argument in the collegiate newspaper. His article dismisses his opponent, now concluding his essay along the lines of "evolution illustrates the non-intelligent design of the universe...," with the implication that being religious (in this case a Mormon) means you couldn't also be rigorously scientific. Such an appeal is called an *ad populum*. Where lies the mistake? Well, for starters, a theory is never true simply because most people happen to believe it. And, of course, being religious (or not) has nothing strictly to do with

---

[5] See also Dan Lips, Shanea Watkins, and John Feming, "Does Spending More on Education Improve Academic Achievement?," in *Backgrounder* (September 8, 2008), and the U.S. Department of Education document *A Nation Accountable: Twenty-Five Years After A Nation at Risk* (Washington, DC, 2008).

being a good empirical scientist. Some scientists are atheists. Others, like Pascal, Newton, Mendel, and Pasteur, are deeply religious. In short, while character counts, it's the claims you should counter. No matter what the crowds say: evaluate the argument, not the speaker.

Good grammar, and reasonable speech, ensure you get the small stuff right. They help you say what you mean, and convince others that you mean what you say. Practice them.

II

Pathos: Proportionate Emotion

Embody Proportio—Move head and heart—
Use vivid language—Prefer the concrete

5. Embody *Proportio*

Pathos refers to the emotional quality of your presentation. You will delight and move your hearers when you bring your listeners' emotions to match your own. One definition of public speaking is simply: "Energetic speech." Your task is, therefore, twofold. You must grasp what emotions naturally correspond to your message. Then you must communicate these convincingly to your audience. You do this by three means: appealing to head and heart, using vivid language, and preferring the concrete. We'll take up the substance of these three here, and add a few details in later chapters.

Before exploring these techniques, however, consider your psychology. Prior to every talk, ask: What emotions ought I to feel? As character is the foundation of style, so proportion—the harmonious relation between parts—is its first manifestation. You must embody *proportio*. How is this achieved?

Ever wonder why a modern city center makes you feel dizzy while a medieval city's core makes you feel cozy? In the old towns of Oxford, Rome, and Quebec, buildings are rarely above three stories high. Streets are wide enough for you to shout across, and be heard. You can walk from one end to the other in under an hour. These cities attract, in a way that Atlanta and Toronto do not, because the parts and the whole correspond to the scale of the human body, not the automobile. These cities manifest *proportio*.

According to the classical understanding, *proportio* makes a thing beautiful because "the senses delight in things duly proportioned."[1] In the visual arts, we call something beautiful when there is a balance between the matter and form, colors and lines, and a thing's scale relative to its intended use. The unease we feel standing beside a New York City project, for example, is not simply because it is tall. Mountains are tall, yet they evoke awe, not revulsion. The aesthetic problem with a Bauhaus-inspired skyscraper apartment is not its enormous mass, at least, not that only; the problem is that its size does not suit the aims of a family home. Skirts look lovely on women, not so good on elephants.

During the 1960s city planners wrongly assumed that poor people would prefer to live in a large building surrounded by a common green rather than a small flat with their own garden. As it turned out, when everybody owns the lawn, nobody owns the lawn—except perhaps for the gangs that move in after dark. The projects were a disaster because the size of the buildings failed to match the normal feelings that one's home is meant to evoke: a sense of privacy, ownership, and intimacy.

When speaking, your emotions, likewise, must match the event. Thus, if you are a football coach giving a talk to the boys between quarters, you might yell. If you are a friend delivering a eulogy after a funeral, you might whisper. Emotions in themselves are neither good nor bad. Emotions are like the keys on a keyboard. Some are high, others low, some flat, some sharp. Obviously, the middle feelings get most use. But even middle C will screech when struck on top of a B major chord. The nature and occasion of your talk provides the score which you must correctly interpret. Get the wrong emotion, and you will look like a skyscraper dropped in the middle of the Piazza Navona.

6. Move head and heart
How to judge which keys to hit? In general, appeal to both head

[1] Thomas Aquinas, *Summa Theologica* I q.5 a.4.

and heart. Let prudence be your guide. Do this and you will avoid two common mistakes. Here is the first. Beginning speakers tend to focus almost exclusively on the logical coherence of their speech, and treat their listeners as though they were talking heads. Your listeners are not talking heads. This is a lesson learned early by one of the greatest orators, Demosthenes.

In the world of ancient Greece, oratory was an essential skill. In the happy days before the IRS, if the government or anybody else took too much from your pie, you didn't usually hire a lawyer. You flashed your sword, or showed up at the Agora to argue your case. As it happened, Demosthenes' father died when he was seven, leaving the boy a huge fortune. His guardians embezzled the funds, sent the tutors home unpaid, and left the child a pauper. As a boy, Demosthenes was sickly. His voice was weak and he was always out of breath. Nevertheless, when he turned twenty he needed the cash, so he marched to court. His first case was a flop. His ancient biographer, Plutarch, relates that his style was overly academic. His speech was encumbered with long sentences and "tortured with formal arguments to a most harsh and disagreeable excess."

Public failures continued. His break seems to have come when his friend Satyrus, who happened to be an actor, followed Demosthenes home one afternoon after another pitiful performance speaking in the courts. Satyrus asked for a text from a play, and got Demosthenes to read it aloud. As usual, his delivery was stilted. His friend asked for the text, and told him to listen, and to watch. Satyrus not only read the words but acted them out. The joy, the sorrow, and the passion of the text leapt off the page and flashed across the face and hands of the actor. Plutarch reports the effect of this lesson on the young Demosthenes:

> …being convinced how much grace and ornament language acquires from action, he began to esteem it a small matter, and as good as nothing for a man to exercise

himself in declaiming, if he neglected enunciation and delivery.[2]

Demosthenes learned a lesson that day that every successful speaker has taken to heart: to convince your listener of what you think you must first *feel* what you say.

Yet as the ancients might say, *nihil nimius*; nothing too much. If ignoring feeling altogether is the first mistake, being overcome by emotion is the second. The problem with too little *pathos* is that it causes you to be ignored. The problem with too much emotion is that it can cause you to be despised.

A humorous example comes to mind. I teach at a college which regularly conducts campus-wide "traditio" days. A few days a term we set everything aside to take up in common some classic text, and then discuss it in seminar.

Our theme one term was "faith and unbelief." Students read the famous 1948 debate between Bertrand Russell and Father Frederick Copleston (the BBC has an archived recording of the event available on the internet). Two faculty members were to act the parts. Students congregated in a large oval surrounding our guests; "Copleston" stood at the north end of the room, "Russell" at the south. The speakers were introduced. The improvised reenactment was engaged. Unfortunately, instructions to the professors were also poor. The two professors—neither very good actors—approached the event from quite different angles. The "atheist" took on the air of an educated, aristocratic Brit (which Russell was), while the "priest" edged closer to the style of a TV evangelist (which Copleston was not). The atheist made his replies with calm composure; the theist starting hurtling *ad hominem* attacks. A good time was had. But, in my view, the wrong side ended up on top. Too much emotion kills credibility. Be proportionate.

---

[2] Plutarch, *Life of Demosthenes*, in *Plutarch's Lives, Volume II*, introduction by James Atlas, trans. John Dryden (NY: The Modern Library, 2001), 391–92.

7. Use vivid language

Vivid language brings clarity and delight. Arthur Koestler's 1940 novel *Darkness at Noon* describes the psychology of a believing Bolshevik, Rubashov, who has been wrongly imprisoned by the party which he serves. Koestler was a Hungarian journalist who emigrated to Britain and fought for the Allies during the Second World War. His account of Soviet political trials was based on the experiences of men he knew directly. The opening description of a prisoner's first impression arrests the reader:

> The cell door slammed behind Rubashov.
> He remained leaning against the door for a few seconds, and lit a cigarette. On the bed to his right lay two fairly clean blankets, and the straw mattress looked newly filled. The washbasin to his left had no plug, but the tap functioned. The can next to it had been freshly disinfected, it did not smell. The walls on both sides were of solid brick, which would stifle the sound of tapping, but where the heating and drain pipe penetrated it, it had been plastered and resounded quite well; besides, the heating pipe itself seemed to be noise-conducting. The window stared at eye-level; one could see down into the courtyard without having to pull oneself up by the bars. So far everything was in order.[3]

The clean blankets, the solid brick wall, and the "freshly disinfected" trash can set the mood for the novel, far more evocatively than would a theoretical account of the horrors of the Soviet prisons. Without telling the reader that "the cell was desolate," Koestler shows directly the camp's brutal, clinical, efficiency. Showing is much better than telling.

---

[3] Arthur Koestler, *Darkness at Noon*, trans. Daphne Hardy (London: Penguin Books, 1947), 9.

Here is another novel's opening. Farley Mowat's depiction of drought on the Canadian plains makes you want to spit the dirt out of your mouth.

> An oppressive darkness shadowed the city of Saskatoon
> on an August day in 1929. By the clock it was hardly
> noon. By the sun—but the earth had obliterated the sun.
> Rising in the new deserts of the southwest, and lifting
> high on autumnal winds, the desecrated soil of the prai-
> ries drifted northward; and the sky grew dark.[4]

Mowat's description pleases because you can see what he describes. Instead of saying, "The prairie began its drought," he shows you what it looked like: blackened sky, high winds, barren fields.

Of course, in speech, vivid language includes more than words. A frown, a lunge, a wave, a whisper: each can add to the clarity of your expression. (We'll take up the physical side of vivid speech in the next chapter when we look at *ethos*.)

8. Prefer the concrete

This leads to the next virtue of emotionally satisfying prose: vivid language is *concrete*. To delight is to move the affections; that is the immediate aim of *pathos*. When you write or speak, therefore, prefer the particular to the general. Tell of the king, the senate, and the dagger, not of the leader, the government, or the weapon.

The following examples illustrate the difference. Below is Portia's famous courtroom speech from Shakespeare's *The Merchant of Venice*. The first is Shakespeare's original, the second rendering has been drained of vivid imagery:

---

[4] Farley Mowat, *The Dog Who Wouldn't Be* (New York: Pyramid Books, 1975), 9.

The quality of mercy is not strain'd,	The nature of mercy does not impose.
It droppeth as the gentle rain from heaven	As a manifestation of the transcendent will
Upon the place beneath: it is twice blest;	It does not abrogate human justice.
It blesseth him that gives and him that takes:	Mercy benefits both the one offering it, And the one who is the beneficiary.
'Tis mightiest in the mightiest: it becomes	It is a quality most praiseworthy when found
The throned monarch better than his crown;	In those with greater socio-economic advantages;
His sceptre shows the force of temp-oral power...	Mercy in government is better than even the efficient deployment of resources...

The image of a sceptre speaks more directly than does "govern-ment." "Droppeth as the gentle rain" forms a picture; "manifesta-tion of the transcendent will" wrinkles the brow. Abstract terms like "beneficiary" and "socio-economic" may find their home somewhere (in dreary textbooks, perhaps?). But you should avoid them.

Pictures, please, and often with fewer words. Note how the mangled example above used 63 words, whereas Shakespeare's required only 46. Concrete language is sturdier, and will carry more meaning with less scaffolding. Brevity satisfies.

That is not, of course, to say that an excellent description need be brief. Here is a selection from Erasmus' account of his friend, Sir Thomas More, then aged forty-one. Notice how Eras-mus piles details on top of each other like the layers of German torte cake:

> You ask me to paint you a full-length portrait of More
> as in a picture. Would that I could do it as perfectly as
> you eagerly desire it. At least I will try to give a sketch of
> the man, as well as from my long familiarity with him I
> have either observed or can now recall. To begin, then,
> with what is least known to you, in stature he is not tall,
> though not remarkably short. His limbs are formed with
> such perfect symmetry as to leave nothing to be desired.

His complexion is white, his face fair rather than pale, and though by no means ruddy, a faint flush of pink appears beneath the whiteness of his skin. His hair is dark brown, or brownish black. The eyes are grayish blue, with some spots, a kind which betokens singular talent, and among the English is considered attractive, whereas Germans generally prefer black. It is said that none are so free from vice.

His countenance is in harmony with his character, being always expressive of an amiable joyousness, and even an incipient laughter, and, to speak candidly, it is better framed for gladness than for gravity and dignity, though without any approach to folly or buffoonery. The right shoulder is a little higher than the left, especially when he walks. This is not a defect of birth, but the result of habit, such as we often contract. In the rest of his person there is nothing to offend. His hands are the least refined part of his body. . . .[5]

Less is not always more. Buildings are not the only cultural works that suffered in the sixties. Language did too. About the time the Beatles started to write songs, a group of linguists concocted a theory that modern people are too dumb to read books older than *Curious George*; so the experts decided to re-write them. In the 1970s, committees began to re-translate, notably, both the Bible and liturgical books.

There is an old metaphysical principle that runs, *corruptio optima pessima*: the corruption of the best is the worst. Nowhere is dull language more damaging than in public prayer. If you are a minister, consider yourself a guardian of language. Before you concoct your own cup of pious pleading, be sure you have drunk deeply of the best that has been spoken.

[5] "Description of Thomas More by Erasmus," taken from a 1519 letter in *Saint Thomas More: Selected Writings*, edited by J. Thornton and S. Varenne, preface by J. Koterski, S.J. (New York: Random House, 2003), 244.

Here is an example of what happens when you don't. After the reform of the Second Vatican Council (1962–65) the Roman Catholic Church updated many of the prayers of the Mass and then ordered new translations from the Latin into the world's vernaculars. The English rendering that came out in the 1970s was intended, apparently, as a stop-gap. The idea was that they would get something out fast, and then provide a proper translation later. I suppose most things Catholic move slowly. The "real" translation only rolled out about forty years after the fact.

The difference between the two translations illustrates the poverty of limp language. In the bell-bottom version much Scriptural imagery is dropped. Prior to receiving communion the faithful are to take upon their lips the words uttered by a noble Roman officer before Christ (Mt. 8:8):

Latin (original): Domine, non sum dignus *ut intres sub tectum meum*: sed tantum dic verbo, et sanabitur *anima mea*.

English translation (1970s): Lord, I am not worthy to receive you, but only say the word and I shall be healed.

English translation (2010): Lord, I am not worthy *that you should enter under my roof*, but only say the word and *my soul* shall be healed.

Note the italics, and what fell out. The 1970s version lost the Biblical allusion. In so doing, it also lost an important tie to history. Prior to the Edict of Toleration, in AD 312, Christians were too busy running from the lions to build churches. For that reason, church gatherings for almost three centuries were held not in public spaces, but in homes. To pray "I am not worthy to have you enter my roof" is to remember not only the devotion of the Roman soldier but also the slaves, accountants, farmers, and pious ladies who, for all those hunted years, opened their homes at the risk of peril to the priest and his mystical guest. To boot, the evocative "*my soul* shall be healed" got hard-boiled down to a lonely "I."

At other points, entire phrases had to be restored, as in the opening prayer of Thursday of the Second Week of Lent:

Latin: Deus, innocentiae restitutor et amator…

English (1970s): God of love…

English (2010): O God, who delight in innocence and restore it…

True, God loves us. But how much more can the mind feast upon when we are told that this God both *delights in innocence* and can *give it back again* when lost! The 2010 translation emotionally satisfies because its language is pictorial, full of allusions, and concrete. In our speech, likewise, each word should sparkle.

If your tradition of worship lacks poets, borrow from another. The Anglican *Book of Common Prayer*, originally published in 1549, is a treasure-house of lush imagery, and worth at least a consultation. Suppose you wish to express regret. Try this model: "Almighty Father, We have erred, and strayed from thy ways like lost sheep, We have followed too much the devices and desires of our own hearts. . . ." Here's another prayer, for peace: "O God, who art the author of peace and lover of concord, in knowledge of whom standeth our eternal life, whose service is perfect freedom: Defend us thy humble servants in all assaults of our enemies. . . ."

These words are from the Office of Morning Prayer and for centuries formed the thoughts of sailors and statesmen of English speakers from General Robert E. Lee to Winston Churchill. It is true that God hears the heart. But, for better or worse, everyone else has to listen to your words. When speaking on behalf of others, use the best you can.

Like the correct use of *logos*, *pathos* will help make your words convince. Order your emotions. Appeal to head and heart. Be vivid. Prefer the concrete.

III

Ethos:
Credible Character

Cultivate the virtues—Don't overstate—
Speak with your body—Move with your motions—
Muster your voice

9. Cultivate the virtues

"Style," it has well been said, is "character embodied in speech."[1] It is the extension of one's personality through space and time. There are skills to learn and tricks to master, but above all it is your self which you must learn to beautify. A sow with lipstick remains a sow; a fool with a blog is still a fool.

The ancient Romans were astute psychologists. Looking back on several hundred years of Greek political experience, as well as their own, they learned that character produces conviction. Quintilian defined the good orator simply as "vir bonus dicendi peritus"—a good man, expert in speech.[2] They knew, while we often forget, that if you wish others to believe you, they must first *like* you, or at least not think you odious. The more you expect from your listener, the more they will require of your character.

Part of the frustrating attraction of Greek tragedies is that they often depict a world with no free actions, or at least a world where fate renders them void. In Sophocles' *Oedipus the King*, for instance, the hero cannot escape the prophesy: his run from doom only leads into the bedroom of his mother. Out of the frying pan into the fire. A man's shoelaces often do feel tied. Sometimes the universe conspires against us; yet, as often as not, the

---

[1] F. L. Lucas, *Style*, 3rd edition (London: Harriman House, 2012), 35.
[2] Quintilian, *Institutes*, 12.1.1.

fates forget their fury and seem to leave us free. After reading an ancient tragedy, or perhaps a play by Kafka, a modern reader may be left wondering: is man free? Or are we simply the playthings of gods, or perhaps our own biology?

Perhaps the answer to this riddle is not "either/or" but "both/and." In other words, even if human beings are subject to outside forces, such as the environment, it at least appears true that we retain the power for some free action. Most great works of literature support this view, as have the majority of philosophers. Aristotle, for example, defines voluntary action as "what has its principle in the agent himself."[3] In this more optimistic view, we are not fated; rather, it is our character that determines the quality of our deeds. And this helps explain why people tend to believe what you say only if they like what you do.

To build character you do not need to be clever. In fact, sometimes sophistication can get in the way of goodness. In your search for inner "Chi" start with what you know. For most of us, that means beginning with what we don't like.

No one likes bad manners. How did you feel last time someone snuck into your parking spot? Or how about when your nephew last forgot to say "thank you"? Men may disagree on metaphysics, but nobody likes to be cheated. On basic morals, on where to begin, there was, until yesterday, wide agreement. Whether you live in Calcutta or in Cincinnati the wisdom of Confucius still stands: "What you don't like done to yourself, don't do to others."

That is only a beginning. Of course, where we should end up can be less clear. When trying to get people to pose for group pictures, a friend of mine in jest often yells something like, "Be natural… No, that's not good enough… Be more natural!" That is the problem. We don't entirely know what it means to *be* natural. We are, we might say, nature's monster. Dogs, cats, sheep, and petunias all act as they are told, by instinct. Men and women

---

[3] Aristotle, *Nichomachean Ethics*, 3.1.20 (trans. Irwin).

make decisions. Decisions repeated form a habit; the sum of your habits adds up to the value of your character. Sooner or later someone you respect is going to ask: What is yours worth?

A virtue is a habit of excellence. It is a tendency that perfects some part of your nature; repeated, it makes you stronger, more what you ought to be. Habits can also flow downstream. Decisions quickly take the form of a second nature. I recall a friend of mine from college who was notorious for being habitually late. Announce the start of a party at 8:00 pm, and he would arrive at 9:30; begin at 9:00 and he would show up at 11:00. By the time he was a junior, it seemed he truly was no longer "free" to be on time. The little time-birdy that chirps for most of us had stopped singing in his ear. His bad habit, unchecked, had become his chain. (Tip: if you have a friend like this, say you hope to see him at the party at 4:00 PM.)

If you want to be excellent at keeping time, or throwing a ball, or completing assignments, you must practice till it becomes second nature. Being punctual, throwing a curve, delivering a B+ paper: these are not the products of genius. They are, for the most part, achievements of steady effort. "But," you ask, "what about being excellent as a human being?" How do the parts relate to the whole?

We are not the first to wonder. Ever noticed how well self-help books sell? They've often got catchy titles like "The 13 Habits" or "Romance 4 Dummies". I've thought of writing one like this: "A Guide to the Virtues: Or, a couple of steps to love, happiness, and a Mercedes-Benz." The title would, in fact, mostly be accurate. Since ancient times philosophers have named four ingredients that every man needs for success. Wait no longer!

Plato famously spoke of the soul as having three parts: reason, will, and desire, along with four chief virtues. The four virtues, the four ingredients for success, map on to the soul from top to bottom. Wisdom, Courage, and Moderation perfect reason, will, and desire. Justice comes when all the parts of the soul work in harmony with each other.

PART OF THE SOUL	VIRTUE
Reason	**Wisdom:** the application of right reason
Will	**Courage:** grit in the face of opposition
Desire	**Moderation:** proportionate appetite
	Justice: harmony within and without

We need other virtues, to be sure—grace, tact, generosity, faith. Still, the four listed above are named "cardinal" because they are literally the hinge (Latin, *cardo*) upon which the rest turn.

Well, perhaps no one can guarantee that the virtues will land you a slick car, but I can promise this: you'll never have a happy romance without them. Consider the case of Darcy and Elizabeth. When the handsome, attractive, rich, and eligible Fitzwilliam Darcy meets Ms. Elizabeth Bennet, heroine of *Pride and Prejudice*, the young cock is stuffed full of pride. Elizabeth, of course, has her own problem (prejudice). Jane Austin's masterful plot shows how only love can provide a motive strong enough to fuel self-transformation. Only Darcy's admiration for Elizabeth moves him to turn pride into noble service; only Elizabeth's regard for Darcy compels her to submit prejudice to reflection. The moral of the story? If you want lasting romance, become worthy of one. Practice the virtues.

You may wonder: what does this have to do with style? A great deal. We tolerate presenters. We suffer lecturers. We are moved by teachers. Think back to your college or high-school years. Can you recall your favorite class? Probably not. Yet you likely *can* still point to a beloved teacher. When you (more than what you say) hold the trust of your listeners, you, that is to say, your character, like a splash of swirling orange juice in a champagne glass, mix with the message.

In a book-length interview with Jorge Bergoglio and the chief rabbi of Buenos Aires, the future Pope Francis drew the connection between ethos and credibility this way:

There is a difference between a professor and a teacher. The professor presents his material in a detached manner, while the teacher involves others; it is profoundly testimonial. There is also coherence between his conduct and his life. He is not merely a transmitter of science, as is a professor. We need to help men and women to become teachers, so that they can become witnesses; that is essential in education.[4]

10. Don't overstate

Becoming a good man satisfies the first half of Quintilian's definition of the good orator. How about the other half? One crucial way by which your character becomes manifest is through the quality of your judgments. Begin by avoiding rash claims. Not all topics are alike. Ask yourself: is this the sort of subject that admits of *certain*, *probable*, or *doubtful* judgments? Before an uneducated audience, this distinction is often blurred. For an educated audience, to keep respect, you must respect the difference.

Here is an illustration. Predicting the cause of changes in sea surface temperatures (SST) is, at this point, a bit like reading tea leaves. It's not that we can't measure SST. It's just that we've only been doing it with any accuracy since about 1967. In the 18th century Ben Franklin dragged a mercury thermometer behind a ship during one of his transatlantic crossings; in the 19th century scientists measured water in buckets of various sizes. In short, over the past 200 years methods have varied widely; however broad, our current samples of SSTs do not go deep. Mapping oceanic temperature variations has a great future. But, since we know so little about the past, any claims you might make about the underlining causes of oceanic temperature variations should be cast as *probable* judgments.

---

[4] Jorge Mario Bergoglio and Abraham Skorka, *On Heaven and Earth* (New York: Image Books, 2013), 132.

The principle holds for the moral sciences, too. You're twenty-two. You've dated for three years. You're close with his parents, his three sisters, his two closest friends. You're confident in his good character. You are in love. Now he proposes. Should you say "no" just because some men cheat? Likely not. The standard of proof must be determined by the nature of the question. In love and romance, you can be prudent, but you cannot avoid risk. Not to marry because you lack absolute certainty is folly. It is otherwise in simple arithmetic. To say that five times five *might* be twenty-five is vice. Arithmetic and romance are both reasonable activities, even though each requires a different method and assumes a different standard of proof.

Or consider it this way. Ever wondered why it is possible for a young man to be a brilliant mathematician, as was Sir Isaac Newton, though only old men can be good historians and statesmen, as was Winston Churchill? The reason is this. Mathematics deals with abstract entities; it requires of us little experience of individual things. Once the terms are defined ("quantity," "addition," "line," and so forth) their essences can be completely grasped. History and statecraft, by contrast, depend upon particulars. Only experience delivers that. Mathematicians correctly expect a high degree of certitude from their study. A commander, on the other hand, must follow, at least sometimes, his best guess.

It seems that sanity itself requires a sense of proportion. The man who can reason from particulars to universal causes is a scientist. The man who knows the facts in front of him is a craftsman. The man who misjudges the facts, but reasons about them consistently, we call a *madman*. Or as G.K. Chesterton memorably put it, "The madman is not the man who has lost his reason. The madman is the man who has lost everything except his reason."[5] Judge wisely, but don't overstate.

---

[5] G.K. Chesterton, *Orthodoxy*, introduction by Philip Yancey (New York: Image Books, 2001), 13.

11. Speak with your body

There is more. We spoke earlier of the power of vivid language. We speak, of course, not only through words. Credible *ethos*—in other words, good character—shines not only through the order of your speech, but also through the vivid motions of your *body*. Learn to speak with it.

Oscar Wilde once quipped, "Only a shallow person does not judge by appearances." And he was right. Dress with dignity. Whatever your close friends might know, everyone else will judge first by how you appear. You might recall your father telling you to cut your hair before you went to your first interview. Maybe it cramped your style; probably it helped you get a job. Follow this rule: if you are the speaker or the leader in the room, dress as well as or better than your peers.

Does wearing a suit and tie stifle authenticity? Not really. First and foremost, it is an act of courtesy. It tends to put your listeners at ease because it signals from the start that you are not going to waste their time. Whenever you speak, you serve the minds of others. When you speak before a group, consider yourself an ambassador for the people to themselves. What do you think they're worth?

That is enough on the drapery. Next, consider how you are going to move it. Many of us have heard that the visual aspect of speech accounts for more than the words. You may have heard from a sales guru that people pay attention to the "3 V's" in the following ratio: 7% to the Verbal message, 38% to the Vocal tone, 55% to the Visual cues. These figures as expressed communicate an overstatement. The numbers were originally derived from two studies by the Iranian psychologist Albert Mehrabian in 1967.[6] Quite helpfully, what Mehrabian's early research indicated was that if any "channel" of communication (or one among the 3 V's) contradicts another, you are more likely to trust the speaker's

---

[6] See his book *Silent Messages: Implicit Communication of Emotions and Attitudes* (Belmont, CA: Wadsworth Publishing Co., 1972).

body than his tone, and his tone more than his words. Unfortunately, the samples his original research included were sex-selective (no men) and analyzed simple interactions that did not mirror real-life situations. Imagine you are at a showroom. A sales man strides confidently up from his desk, shakes your hand, gazes pleasingly, and motions expertly to have you join him in his office. He may please for a moment. Eventually, though, his words will catch up. If a message lacks substance, the pitch usually won't sell. So long as listeners retain their wits, rational speech retains a priority.

Still, the body counts. And, truth be told, we often do lose our wits. To understand the meaning of movement, and what the body tells, we need to acquire the art of observation. Books can help, but your own observations serve best.

The language of your body will tell your audience whether or not what you say is credible. Before they listen to you, people will *watch* to see if you are telling them the truth. When asked how he always got his man, in a candid moment, Sherlock Holmes—that master of human motivation—revealed the secret to his power of deduction: he listened, but, since men often lie, he learned also how to look:

> By a man's finger-nails, by his coat-sleeve, by his boot,
> by his trouser-knees, by the callosities of his forefinger
> and thumb, by his expression, by his shirt-cuffs—by
> each of these things a man's calling is plainly revealed.
> That all united should fail to enlighten the competent
> enquirer in any case is almost inconceivable.[7]

You may never solve a crime, but you'll often play the detective. What matters most is that you learn to do better with the clues that you can find (and send the right hints to others).

On balance, women hold the advantage. During the courting

---

[7] Arthur Conan Doyle, "A Study in Scarlet," in the *Adventures of Sherlock Holmes*, ed. Edgar W. Smith (New York: Heritage Press, 1950), 16.

phase, men are often hopelessly outclassed by the lasses, incapable of catching even the most not-so-subtle of hints. In the domestic sphere, too, men often report how hard it is to hide something from their wives. For whatever it's worth, my wife seems to have four eyes. All of them are beautiful, of course, but each one too quick for me. She loves surprises. I find it nearly impossible to deliver them.

On a certain Mother's Day not long ago, I had determined I would bring home a bright, lush hanging basket of petunias for the front porch. I left late. I returned after dark. I hid the precious parcel along the side of the house. I looked forward to watching her surprised expression that lovely May morning. Well, before the lights were out my plot was uncovered. Next year I'll have to try bulbs.

Evidently, if you carry such a handicap you are not alone. A set of researchers at Harvard University wanted to see if they could verify whether women indeed read non-verbal cues better than men. Here's what they found. The team funneled individuals through a darkened room where they showed a short movie clip of a man and a woman interacting. They turned off the sound and asked the individuals what the scene portrayed. Whereas only 42% of the men correctly deciphered the meaning, 87% of women succeeded.[8] Take heart. Even if you're as observant as a doorknob, you can always become a better doorknob.

When learning the language of the body, begin with what you know. While we're on romance, imagine for a moment the different ways that a man may address his wife with the words "Yes, dear." There is the steely "Yes, dear" spit out from a clenched jaw in the heat of an argument; there is the playful "Yes, dear?" which asks a question about the evening's romance. Then, at last, there is the hurried "Yes, dear" tossed over the shoulder while stumbling out of the door to work. The text is the same. It

---

[8] The study is reported in B. and A. Pease, *The Definitive Book of Body Language* (New York: Bantam Books, 2004), 13.

is the tone, expression, volume, and gesture that will charge the message: as call to war, a call to love, or even a call to escape. Whether you like it or not, beyond the bare words, we each employ another language, the language of the body. It is worth mastering the grammar.

12. Move with your motions

There are three basic types of bodily motion: change of position; change of motion; change of velocity. Again, the goal is natural speech. Reflecting on your body helps you become conscious of how it already communicates.

Change of position. The first refers to the change across two dimensions of space, or the floor plan. Most often you will wish to walk within one of three patterns:

the Box;

the Pace;

or the Prowl.

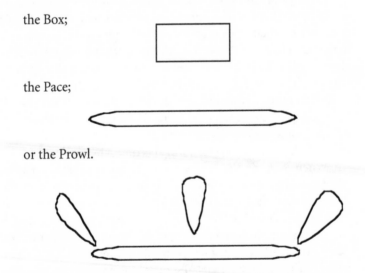

In general, you should walk or stand in a way that feels natural. Motion attracts the eye, and hence the attention. The more excited you are the more you will tend to roam. Roam too much (I once attended a conference where the speaker ran a lap around the entire auditorium!) and you risk looking silly. Move too little, and you look stiff. Practice and conscious reflection will be your best guides.

When you begin, follow this rule of thumb. Limit your steps to a 3 x 3 x 3-foot Box. This gives you enough space to interact with various parts of the room, without wearing yourself out or wandering away. The Pace is useful when your room is shallow and wide. Occasionally pacing between one side of the room and the other can help to retain the focus of those seated along the peripheries.

Prowl with caution. Consider your past experience. It works best with the young. If you are explaining instructions for an overnight hike to a group of campers, you're likely to stroll in-between and around your troop to keep them alert. It can also help a sleepy crowd of adults keep their lids open. Be cautious: if your words are limp, running like a basketball player across the floor will only annoy. The times I have seen ministers walk up and down the aisle when delivering their sermons, I have usually felt that their extra effort would have been better spent on preparation the night before. Start with the Box.

Change of motion. Your position determines where your audience will look; the motion of your face, hands, and limbs regulates what they will see. Most important is your face. We are complex. Our basic appetites, however, are simple. They can be reduced to two: attraction and revulsion. All other emotions, we might say, are variations on the theme.

Here we need to recall an old observation of applied psychology. We mentioned earlier the soul's three "parts." Not literally, of course (an immaterial thing cannot be divided). What the pre-Freudian psychologists meant is that the soul expresses three kinds of *activities*. There is the activity of the intellect, of the will, and of the desires. With the first we think, and with the second we choose; the third corresponds to unreflective impulses. Multiply these three parts of the soul by the two appetites, and that leaves a sum of six elementary contrary expressions.

Part of Soul	Attraction	Revulsion
Reason	Certainty	Doubt
Will	Love	Fear
Desire	Joy	Sadness

Learn to convey each convincingly. Certainty and doubt pertain most to the intellect, and accordingly require more subtle expression. Since love and fear pertain to the will, their expression is more vigorous. Lastly, there is joy and sadness. The face can express more emotions than these, but no fewer!

Consider the other ways your face speaks. To indicate approval, we nod, disapproval, we shake; when we are less interested, or perhaps ashamed, our eyes shift; when we are determined, we stare directly. Like it or not, to speak convincingly you need to learn how to act... at least a little.

If acting does not come *secundum naturam*, as second nature, do not fear. Try watching a few minutes from a classic movie without the sound. Record how often these six basic emotions flash before you. Notice how actors exaggerate. It's Hollywood, but in this case it's somewhat true to life. Natural expression is your aim. To communicate before an audience, however, requires amplification. Singers learn the same secret. What will feel like a large frown to you will hardly be noticed by the man sitting at the back of the hall—that is, unless you magnify your features. Study actors. Practice in front of a mirror. Then be natural.

A final observation, on the eyes. It is almost always best to look directly at someone when you speak. You have likely been in a class or a board-room where the leader of the assembly seemed to speak about eighteen inches above everybody's head. Avoid this. It communicates lack of interest, fear, dishonesty, or all three. If you cannot look at everybody, land your gaze on *somebody*. When you look at one person even for a moment a connection will vicariously be felt by every person.

There are two basic patterns for your eyes to follow. The first is the Sweep. You accomplish this by sweeping your vision from side (A) to side (B) of the room.

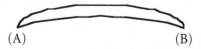

(A)   (B)

The sweep of your eye offers similar benefits to those of the Pace, though without an invasive or aggressive motion. Move your eyes at regular intervals, neither quickly nor slowly.

The second pattern is the Horseshoe. When the room is deep you will want to move your visual attention from the front left quadrant, to the back left, to the back right, to the front right, and then around again. Pause between each lap. Let your eyes rest on one individual, and speak to him personally. Then, move along.

Change of velocity. Here the focus is on the hands. They tell more than you think. A former FBI agent's account of how he cracked a tragic crime illustrates this:[9]

> A suspect in the case was brought in for questioning. His words sounded convincing and his story was plausible. He claimed he hadn't seen the victim and while out in a field had gone down a row of cotton, turned left, and

[9] Joe Navarro, *What Every Body is Saying: An Ex-FBI Agent's Guide to Speed-Reading People* (New York: Collins Publishers, 2008), 4.

then walked straight to his house. While my colleagues jotted down notes about what they were hearing, I kept my eyes on the suspect and saw that as he told the story about turning left and going home, his hand gestured to his right, which was exactly the direction that led to the rape scene. If I hadn't been watching him, I wouldn't have caught the discrepancy between his verbal ("I went left") and nonverbal (hand gesturing to the right) behavior. But once I saw it I suspected he was lying. I waited a while and then confronted him again, and in the end he confessed to the crime.

Moderation is the key. Individuals and even entire cultures have their own pace. Arabs and Italians wave their exclamation marks in front of your nose. Brits keep their hands to themselves. In America, styles mix. Respect your temperament, but become conscious. Study the conductor the next time you listen to an orchestra or worship in a church with a choir. Follow their motions. Then practice.

13. Muster your voice

Your voice, like your limbs, is like any other instrument. If you wish to play it well, you must play it often. You have no excuse.
Your aim, remember, need not be to perform at Carnegie Hall; it is simply to have your sound match your emotions. The three basic alterations of your voice are: in your *tempo* (from slow to fast), in your *pitch* (from high to low), and in your *projection* (from soft to loud).

A moderate volume, pace, and pitch is typical of conversational speech. This is the norm against which listeners will judge you. Any variation from conversational speech will communicate emphasis. Again, do not look for a mechanical formula. Typically, when you come to what is most important, your voice will rise. At other times, you may wish to whisper, or slow down. Get used to silent pauses. Most people can comfortably read a text at about 100 words per minute. Speak much faster and you will become difficult to understand; much slower, and you may bore. Variation is the one rule. Listen to those speakers whom you like. Find novels on CD from your library. Classic British and American books are often read by actors who have mastered the art of pleasant speech.

"Aha!," you protest. "I knew I could never speak in public. *My voice* is weak." Well, join the club. History is full of speakers who overcame their impediments. You can too. Remember Demosthenes's lungs? When he spoke, people wouldn't listen, in part, because they couldn't hear what he said. He knew he had something to say. It is said he placed pebbles in his mouth and then rehearsed his speeches at the edge of the Aegean Sea, till he could be heard. St. Bernardine of Sienna was one of Italy's greatest itinerant preachers. His voice was naturally weak, and croaked. He was called to preach, however, so he did. Eventually, crowds would travel far and arrive early when they knew he was passing through. He spoke inside and out, at times to crowds of up to 30,000 (no microphone, thanks). Churchill started out with a lisp. Actor James Earl Jones began with a stutter. If you want to see how King George VI overcame his speech impediment, you can watch *The King's Speech*. The point is: native ability counts for little of your ultimate success.

Besides simply speaking, simple exercises are best. Here is one I like. Learn to sing the scale: do, re, mi, fa, sol, la, ti, do. Next time you're near a piano you can plunk it out.

Try this exercise five times each morning for a month, and the tone of your voice, as well as your endurance, will improve. In the rhetoric course I teach we begin each class with a short song.

It's good fun. But it also helps my students recognize that good speaking, just like good singing, comes from your belly. If this is difficult, take ten deep breaths when you get up, and then again before bed; do the same two minutes before you are slotted to speak.

Next to your face, your voice is your most communicative instrument. It's helpful to know how to use it, and equally how to relax it. I am one of those lucky few who don't despair of speaking in public. I only *feel* nauseous. Not long ago I was preparing for an interview. Technical problems caused a delay, which meant more time for a cramped stomach. So I started to walk around the room and quietly to sing to myself. It is perfectly possible the interviewer will never invite me back. But we do not need to be shy. If you are odd enough to agree to speak in public, you're probably odd enough to sing quietly to yourself. Start with the scale.

However you speak, and in whatever context you speak, aim for your voice, face, and limbs to convey what you feel. If you are convinced, others likely will be too.

IV

The Aims of the Speaker

Begin from ends—
Match means to ends

14. Begin from ends

You've grasped the three means of persuasion. Now, how do you begin to organize your thoughts? You begin from the ends, that is to say, from your purposes, and then work backwards.

Three immediate ends are possible. You will wish either *to teach*, *to please*, or *to move*. In other words, your aim will be to inform, to give delight, or to incite action. Of these three aims teaching is the most important. If your hearer cannot understand what you intend to communicate, they cannot even disagree, let alone act upon what you suggest. To teach is to make clear what was obscure; it is the bottom rung of the ladder every speaker must scale. Rational argumentation (e.g., clear thesis, structure, definitions, etc.) comes first.

Since man is rational, any truth you present will please. Man is not, however, merely rational. Truth unadorned is often ignored. Consider how, over the period of a day, one of your listeners may have experienced eight hours at work prior to listening to you. Sleep went sour at 5:00 AM last morning. At noon her arthritis flared. On the way home, she lost her keys. Her husband forgot to heat the chicken. Over supper she fought with her daughter. And now she must make the effort to put these things aside to listen to you. To serve your audience well, you must please them, if only by being pleasant. Jokes, anecdotes, and brevity all add to delight. Most importantly, though, don't waste people's time. Come prepared. End when you promise. Since movement adds interest, a tough audience (or a younger one) may need to see emotion not only on your face but also in the articulation of your hands. The less educated, the younger, or the less interested your audience, the more you will need to work to please them.

To prepare for your talk, imagine the mood and expectations of those whom you are about to face. For instance, if you are addressing a group of employees on Friday afternoon, your audience is ready to go home. Earn their hearing. Ask: How can I place my colleagues in a better frame of mind? It's usually not magic. Consider what would please you if you sat in your listener's position. Perhaps you might set out coffee. Maybe you should order tea and fruit. Make sure everyone can perch on a comfortable chair. Courtesy may not carry us to the peaks of charity, but it can carry us to its foothills. In general, the more you wish to please, the more you must attend to the senses, not least through vivid, concrete language.

So much for teaching and pleasing. At other times you will need to carry your listeners farther, to action.

The first step is to make concrete the implication of your claims. Say directly what you wish them to do. Imagine you are a manager at a small construction company. Summer brings more work and hotter days. For the good of all, you wish to change the hours of your crew's operation. Say so directly. Instead of "We ought to get moving a bit earlier in the day," say: "I would like us to be at the site by 6:00 am." You will not always be in a position to command assent. Even if you have the authority to alter someone's routine, usually you will wish either to consult him first or to provide reasons for your decision. Whereas lecturers tend to remain at the level of principle, the talk of a gym teacher, a politician, a preacher, or a parent must be direct.

Often, but not always, to move you must use simple language. This does not mean that you must speak simplistically, but merely bear in mind that a non-athletic or "civilian" audience has a farther emotional distance to travel than one already primed for activity, like a basketball team. The more concise your words, the more memorable they are likely to be:

Fourscore and seven years ago our fathers brought forth on this continent a new nation, conceived in liberty, and dedicated to the proposition that all men are created equal. Now we are engaged in a great civil war, testing whether that nation, or any nation so conceived and so dedicated can long endure...

Lincoln's *Gettysburg Address* of November 19, 1863, delivered just months after the Union forces defeated the Confederate army at Gettysburg, Pennsylvania, accomplished a remarkable range of objectives in just ten sentences: it outlined the origin of America and its founding principles; it rendered praise to those who perished in the country's defense; it aimed to inspire the citizenry to secure the gains of war. His words were simple, not simplistic.

15. Match means to ends

Once you've established your end—whether you wish primarily to teach, please, or move—you can turn to technique. Here enters a complicating factor: you are not the only party involved. To get a complete picture of your talk's objectives you must broaden your view to include the audience's perspective. After all, if the room were empty, would you open your mouth?

To match means to ends pay your respects to what is called the "communication triangle." It's a device for clarifying your end (and hence determining your methods or rhetorical techniques) based on an observation that goes back to Aristotle's *Rhetoric*. Aristotle's advice for determining the content of your speech, your delivery, and your devices was to look to your audience. As he wrote, "the hearer determines the speech's end or object."[1] He does not mean that a speaker must act like a paid client. Rather, the hearer determines your end inasmuch as it is the hearer whom you wish to teach, please, or move.

---

[1] Aristotle, *Rhetoric*, 1.3. (trans. Ross)

To specify the end or objectives of the talk, consider these "pylons" or points of the triangle within which you must work: the authority you carry as *speaker*, the message within your general *subject*, as well as the expectations of your *hearers*.

Speaker (*ethos*)

Subject (*logos*)   Hearer (*pathos*)

Let's take the first two points of the triangle together. First, what is your authority? Second, what's the nature of the subject you wish to address? "Fourscore and seven" is a little stilted for most speeches. Even in Lincoln's day, his introduction signaled an elevated subject. He was there to speak of the Civil War and of Reconstruction. The level of your oratory, the degree of rhetorical flourish you employ, will be determined not only by the proximate aim of your allocution (to teach, to delight, or to move), but also its subject matter (economy, war, heaven), and your position (teacher, politician, preacher). Your task is to judge how close to each of the pylons you will stand. For instance, presidential speeches, orations on war and peace, and perhaps even the opening of an important board meeting must be clothed with formal elements associated with what is called the "grand style," as Lincoln's was. Lincoln's elevated language matched the subject, the occasion, and his authority as president.

To take another scenario, consider the different feelings that two preachers evoke. One speaks on a street corner, the other from a pulpit. Even if they read an identical script, the first causes initial ill-ease, which the second does not. Speechifiers at the corner of London's Hyde Park (the sight of the famous Speaker's Corner) can give off the air of quackery. This is not necessarily because of what they say but because of their lack of social authorization to say it. I hold nothing against street preachers. Some of our drab downtowns would be far more interesting if we had more of them. The point is that context counts. Know yourself and what your audience can reasonably expect from you.

Postmodern people tend to be suspicious of claims to authority. This is an unfortunate habit. Authority is inescapable. Each one of us bears some measure of it. The question is not whether or not we should seize authority, but how we will use the authority we have for the good. No doubt authority can be abused. But much of the evil and sadness in our time can be attributed to the lack of the exercise of authority.

St. Augustine, perhaps the greater Christian preacher after St. Paul, was someone who knew the value of authority and used it well. In his teaching manual, he relates a moving account of how he helped bring peace to a warring city. Gang violence is nothing new. Augustine was bishop of Hippo, a city in modern Algeria, then of about the same size and importance as Plum Creek, Alabama. Apparently, in a neighboring city, old feuds within the community would flare up once a year. Citizens would break into gangs, slaughter one another for several days, and then return to work before the next year's killings. Think 1990s Kosovo. Augustine heard of the perverse custom and determined to put it to a stop. Here's how he did it.

He began with his hearers. They were at war, and he wished to stop it. That determined the "style" of rhetoric he would use. It was to be "grand." He then sized up his position. He was a bishop. Some today still respect bishops. In those days, you had no choice. His position was somewhere between spiritual guru and town magistrate. As bishop, Augustine used his authority to advantage and called a public meeting. The people gathered. Then, given his aim, his audience, and his position, he spoke, as he says, "to the best of my ability, in the grand style." And it worked. By his words, he was able to reduce his audience to repentance. The violence never returned. As he later reflected on the experience:

I did not think I had achieved anything when I heard
them applaud, but only when I saw them in tears. Their
applause showed that they were receiving instruction
and experiencing delight; their tears that they were
moved.[2]

Stopping wars is not for ninnies. Few of us are likely to have such
a privileged task. Yet, each of us is called, now and again, as St.
Francis of Assisi was, to bring peace where there is strife and joy
where there is hatred.

If Augustine were alive today, my guess is that he too would
occasionally get stuck in traffic. He might find himself caught
somewhere between Boston and New York, in a traffic jam,
where he might read the phrase "Co-Exist" on a bumper sticker.
An hour later, now nearly through Connecticut on I-95, he
would hit another bottleneck. This time he reads "Question
Authority." I imagine he would wonder why people don't question the authority of those who question authority. Presumably,
in the next world, men will not have to exercise authority. Here it
seems we cannot live without it.

Nearing the end of his journey Augustine, I imagine, would
think more nice thoughts—of the duties of ministry, and of
manhood. He would step out of his car to speak at a youth conference, on apologetics. Lines from Taylor Mali's sardonic poem
"Totally like whatever, you know" would then flood his mind:

What has happened to our conviction?
Where are the limbs out on which we once walked?
Have they been, like, chopped down
with the rest of the rain forest?
Or do we have, like, nothing to say?
Has society become so, like, totally…

[2] St. Augustine, *On Christian Teaching*, trans. R.P.H. Green (Oxford: OUP,
1997), 4.139–40.

I mean absolutely... You know?
That we've just gotten to the point where it's just, like...
whatever!

Because contrary to the wisdom of the bumper sticker,
it is not enough these days to simply QUESTION
AUTHORITY.
You have to speak with it, too.

Don't fool yourself. Even within a democracy, all men are not equal. Am I addressing my peers, my betters, or my subordinates? Am I a citizen among citizens, an employee among employees, a teacher among teachers? Consider carefully, and in the widest aspect, your ends. Only then can you turn to the question of means.

Your "means" encompass the kinds of techniques you will employ, your emotional pitch, the sorts of examples you will evoke, the kind of logical appeals you will make. Though Augustine and Lincoln both used the "grand style," more typically you will deploy—or give the appearance of deploying—fewer rather than more rhetorical devices. Rhetoricians call this "the mixed style." When you speak on less emotive subjects, and before your peers, use "the restrained style." In an approximate way, these three levels of oratory relate to the points of the communication triangle. Consider the following *rough* guide.

Subject & Object	Level	+	Hearer	=	Speaker's Aim
Academic Topics	Private		to teach		Restrained
Theoretical or practical	Semi-public		to please		Mixed
Practical matters	Public		to move		Grand

Your ingenuity and your sweat do count. But to persuade others, you must learn to submit yourself—your ambitions, your personality—to the purpose of your talk. You are there to serve. Respect the triangle. Match means to ends.

V

The Structure of a Speech

Perfect the essay—Open with a hook—
Mark transitions

16. Perfect the essay

You've learned the motives of persuasion. You've identified your audience. Your aims are clear. It is now time to organize the sequence of your thoughts. Speech comes first in experience; usually, though, we become conscious of the forms and structures of our speech once we put pen to paper. We'll begin, then, with that most elegant and elementary form of communication, the essay.

"[T]he essay," wrote Aldous Huxley, "is a literary device for saying almost everything about almost anything."[1] Derived from the French, it literally means an *attempt* (*l'essay*). Attempt at what? Michel de Montaigne (1533–92) was the form's first master. His essays are an effort at drawing the reader's mind to his own. Their virtue lies in their simplicity. A good essay is like a good pair of glasses. It aims not to be seen, but to make clear. Montaigne observed, "When eloquence draws attention to itself it does wrong by the substance of *things*."[2] Words are to lead us to things. As a form, an expository essay has one theme. When you write, therefore, you wish your words to carry your reader to one great thing. Every vista along the path ought gently to prepare the eye for its final destination. Your trip, then, will have three phases: the introduction, the body, and the conclusion. Since missteps come most often at the beginning, we'll spend extra time there.

---

[1] Aldous Huxley, *Collected Essays* (New York: Harper and Row, 1971), v.
[2] Montaigne, "On Educating Children," in *The Essays: A Selection*, trans. M.A. Screech (London: Penguin, 2004), 68.

Before we set out, let me clarify what I am not saying. I do not propose that every sermon should sound like a *New York Times* op-ed. Nor do I deny the virtue of story-telling. But preachers, politicians, and poets, like everybody else, need to be clear if they wish to compel. The essay can teach you how to achieve this.

17. Open with a hook

We begin at the beginning. The purpose of the introduction is to convince your reader (or listener) to keep going. If you fail at this, you succeed at nothing. You keep them reading by three means: the hook, the line, and the sinker.

The *hook* grabs attention. It identifies the value of your topic. Here are common devices.

You might begin with a surprising statistic:

> In the 1950s, the birth rate in America reached 3.8 live births per woman; today it is 1.9.

Or:

> As was recently reported by the Centers for Disease Control and Prevention, since 1988 the use of antidepressant drugs in the US increased nearly 400%.[3]

You might open with a question:

> Is it true that beauty lies only in the eye of the beholder?

Or:

---

[3] Centers for Disease Control and Prevention, "Antidepressant Use in Persons Aged 12 and Over: United States, 2005–2008," *NCHS Data Brief* (Number 76), October 2011.

Do you know what causes great nations to lose wars?
(It's not usually a lack of arms.)

You might tell an apt story:

Imagine your school in three years. Enrollment is up
15%. You've doubled your endowment. Faculty are
enthusiastic about your mission. Let me tell you about
one school where this happened...

Or:

Once, when General Dwight D. Eisenhower was under
siege, he sent a sergeant out to do some reconnaissance.
When he returned, the General said, "Sergeant, give me
a brief assessment of our position." The sergeant replied,
"Sir, imagine a doughnut. We're the hole."[4]

In formal or academic writing, it is more typical to state the topic
of your essay and its value directly. I've italicized the hook:

The subject of this essay is not the so-called "liberty of
the will," so unfortunately opposed to the misnamed
doctrine of philosophical necessity; but civil, or social
liberty: the nature and limits of the power which can be
legitimately exercised by society over the individual. A
question seldom stated, and hardly ever discussed in
general terms, but *which profoundly influences the practical controversies of the age by its latent presence* and is
likely soon to make itself recognized as the vital question
of the future. (John Stuart Mill, *On Liberty*)[5]

---

[4] See Meyers and Nix, *As We Speak: How to Make Your Point and Have it Stick*
(New York: Atria Books, 2011), 58.

[5] John Stuart Mill's *On Liberty* (1859) (London: Penguin, 1974), 59.

Or:

> Intelligent life on a planet comes of age when it first
> works out the reason for its own existence. If superior
> creatures from space ever visit earth, the first question
> they will ask, in order to assess the level of our civiliza-
> tion, is: "Have they discovered evolution yet?" Living
> organisms had existed on earth, without ever knowing
> why, for over three thousand million years before the
> truth finally dawned on one of them. His name was
> Charles Darwin. . . . My purpose is to examine the biol-
> ogy of selfishness and altruism. . . . Apart from its aca-
> demic interest, *the human importance of this subject is
> obvious. It touches every aspect of our social lives,* our lov-
> ing and hating, fighting and cooperating, giving and
> stealing, our greed and our generosity. (Richard Dawk-
> ins, *The Selfish Gene*)[6]

The *absence* of a formal introduction can, on rare occasions, grab your reader's attention. Take a second look at the opening to Caesar's *Gallic War*. This time, observe how he begins *in media res*, in the middle of the action:

> The whole of Gaul is divided into three parts, one of
> which the Belgae inhabit, the Aquintani another, and the
> third a people who in their own language are called
> "Celts," but in ours, "Gauls." They all differ among
> themselves in respect of language, way of life, and laws.

I regularly wrangle with students who were taught that their introduction needs to be "creative." Don't make that mistake. Open with a fact, ask a question, tell a story, or state the value of your topic directly; then move on.

[6] Richard Dawkins, *The Selfish Gene* (Oxford: Oxford University Press, 1989), 1–2.

If the hook generates interest, the *line* leads your reader to a definite point. If you cannot reduce your thesis to a single statement, your essay or your speech is probably not worth making: it likely won't be understood; it certainly won't be remembered.

Every essay, every speech, is like a symphony. It is comprised of various parts, but governed by a single theme. What is yours? In 1954, Sir Winston Churchill, then 84 years old, visited Washington, DC. He attended a talk given by a prominent US political leader. Afterwards, the speaker asked Churchill for feedback on his address. "In all candor," Churchill replied, "the impact of your talk was [pause] underwhelming. You spoke of NATO, the need for reciprocity in trade, the importance of the Anglo-American alliance, but it had no theme."[7] Make sure yours has a theme.

The best "line" is a thesis statement, a single proposition which your essay aims to support. On some occasions, however, a statement of the subject or even of the purpose of your writing may substitute for the thesis. In such a case, signal to your reader that they must look elsewhere for your thesis—usually in the conclusion. The chief advantage of this technique is that it builds the reader's expectation. C.S. Lewis employed this sort of line in his opening chapter to *The Problem of Pain*:

> At all times, then, an inference from the course of events in this world to the goodness and wisdom of the Creator would have been equally preposterous; and it was never made. Religion has a different origin. In what follows it must be understood that I am not primarily arguing the truth of Christianity but describing its origin—a task, in my view, necessary if we are to put the problem of pain in its right setting.[8]

[7] Related by James C. Humes in *The Sir Winston Method* (New York: William Morrow and Company, 1991), 44.

[8] C.S. Lewis, *The Problem of Pain*, in *C.S. Lewis: Selected Books* (London: HarperCollins, 1999), 475.

See if you can spot the kinds of "line" employed by Mill and Dawkins, respectively, in the previous examples.

Lastly, the *sinker*. Having gained the ear of your reader or audience, say how long you wish to keep it. Tell them where you wish to go, and they will be more willing to follow. Here are the openings of two very different self-help books:

> In writing about painting in these short books, we will, to make our discourse clearer, first take from mathematicians those things which seem relevant to the subject. When we have learned these, we will go on, to the best of our ability, to explain the art of painting from the basic principles of nature. (Leon Battista Alberti, *On Painting*, 1.1)[9]

> Each of the temperaments has certain communication strengths and weaknesses. In the next four chapters, we present some real-life challenges couples have faced in their marriage.... We also present some tried-and-true communication skills that can help prevent and resolve some of these communication problems. (A. and L. Bennett, *The Temperament God Gave Your Spouse*)[10]

The sinker tells your reader what to expect. It gives them confidence that you are a trustworthy guide. From the opening of the marriage book, you know that: (1) you will encounter examples of difficulties that other couples have faced; and (2) you will learn habits that help you negotiate them. Reading an essay, like listening to a speech, is an investment of time. Your audience wants to be assured that it will be worth theirs.

---

[9] Alberti, *On Painting* (1436), trans. Cecil Grayson, introduction and notes by M. Kemp (London: Penguin, 2004), 37.
[10] Opening to chapter three of A. and L. Bennett's *The Temperament God Gave Your Spouse* (Manchester, NH: Sophia Press, 2008).

Your introduction builds the foundation for your essay. Devote time to building well. If you have five hours to write, likely you should devote at least one to your introduction.

I have the pleasure of teaching good students. Still, I like to remind them on occasion that if I weren't being paid, I'd quit reading after suffering through most of their introductions. Take a look at this sample:

> "Many are the wonders, none is more wonderful than what is man." So proclaims the Chorus in Sophocles' tragic play, *Antigone*, and there is great truth in this. Man is not a simple creature; he is a living paradox, having the capacity within his nature for the most profound extremes—the most noble good and the most terrible evil, the most glorious happiness and the most wretched misery. We are reminded of this truth continuously throughout the play, for a tragedy is so beautiful precisely because it shows us true humanity through these extremes, but it is particularly meaningful for the play's central character, Creon. Creon is the main character, the tragic hero, of the play because, as Aristotle defines it in his work *Poetics*, a tragedy is "an imitation of an action," and the action of this tragedy is Creon's.

This student has talent. But her introduction was weak. You are left to wonder: What's her claim? Where is she taking us? For how long? Of course, she revised (see below). Her additions are in bold; her reflective comments for the purpose of our writing class are in italics.

> "Many are the wonders, none is more wonderful than what is man." So proclaims the Chorus in Sophocles' tragic play, *Antigone*, and there is great truth in this. Man is not a simple creature; he is a living paradox, having the capacity within his nature for the most profound

extremes—the most noble good and the most terrible evil, the most glorious happiness and the most wretched misery. **We witness these extremes** [*Changed passive verb to active and object to match*] continuously throughout *Antigone*, but **we can see them particularly** in the play's **tragic hero, Creon.** [*I changed "the play" to "Antigone" to avoid repetition. I increased the sense of parallelism for "We witness these human extremes…" by replacing "it is particularly meaningful…" with "we can see them…".*…] **At the beginning, Creon is the new, well-respected ruler of Thebes; by the end, he has failed in his office and his beloved wife and son are dead.** [*I brought this element from the conclusion to complete the hook.*] **How does he come to this terrible end? Creon ends tragically because he makes the good of the polis his highest good. To show this, I will examine first the reasons for his initial action, then the flaw in his reasoning, and, finally, how this flaw leads to his ruin.** [*I did not have the line or the sinker, so I had to add these last few sentences.*]

Much better, wouldn't you agree?

18. Mark transitions

After the introduction comes the body. The body of your paper is a whole divided by logical parts. This is where you convincingly develop your case. Each paragraph (or group of paragraphs) should advance a claim, and each claim should support your thesis. It is in the body of the essay that you offer your evidence, your examples, your illustrations; where you identify possible applications of your thesis, and sometimes raise and answer objections. Transitions mark each part. We will start with the divisions within paragraphs, and then between paragraphs, taking up the concluding paragraph last.

Within the paragraph

Say it, illustrate it, argue it, say it again. It was an old habit already observed and recommended by Aristotle.[11] Once you notice the pattern, you'll come to see how consistently good communicators follow this template. Here's an acronym: CERC —claim, example, reason, claim. Sometimes, the position of the example and the reason will be reversed. (And sometimes, as below, even a good writer may break up into two paragraphs what logically belongs to a single paragraph.) See if you can spot Niccolò Machiavelli's movement in this excerpt near the beginning of *The Prince*:

> I say, then, that in hereditary states accustomed to the bloodline of their prince the difficulties in maintaining them are much less than in new states because it is enough only not to depart from the order of his ancestors, and then to temporize in the face of accidents. In this way, if such a prince is of ordinary industry, he will always maintain himself in his state unless there is an extraordinary and excessive force which deprives him of it; and should he be deprived of it, if any mishap whatever befalls the occupier, he reacquires it.
>
> We have in Italy, for example, the duke of Ferrara, who, for no other cause than that his line was ancient in that dominion, did not succumb to the attacks of the Venetians. . . . In the antiquity and continuity of the dominion the memories and causes of innovations are eliminated. . . .[12]

Between paragraphs

Transitions between paragraphs signal a shift in the direction of your argument. They mark the progress of your thought and keep your reader from feeling lost.

---

[11] See his *Rhetoric to Alexander*, 1438b.

[12] Machiavelli, *The Prince*, trans. Harvey C. Mansfield, second edition (Chicago: University of Chicago Press, 1998), 6–7.

There is the numerical sequence:

First...
Second...
Third...

You can begin or end a paragraph with a question or answer (with Locke, below, his question is asked rhetorically):

Can the deficit be reduced? I believe it can.

Or:

> May the Commands then of a Prince be opposed? May
> he be resisted as often as any one shall find himself
> aggrieved, and but imagine he has not Right done him?
> This will unhinge and overturn all Polities, and instead
> of Government and Order, leave nothing but Anarchy
> and Confusion. (John Locke, *Second Treatise on Govern-
> ment*, 18.203)

You might briefly sum up your last topic and introduce your next:

> ...who pose as good men at the moment of greatest per-
> fidy. But enough has now been said about Justice. Our
> Next topic as earlier proposed is to be munificence or
> generosity. Nothing more accords with human nature as
> this.... (Cicero, *On Obligations*, 1.41–42; trans. Walsh)

Or:

> From Venus, the carnal ingredient within Eros, I now
> turn to Eros as a whole. Here we shall see the same pat-
> tern repeated. As Venus within Eros does not really aim

at pleasure, so Eros does not really aim at happiness.
(C.S. Lewis, *The Four Loves*)[13]

Or:

But such distinctions are more appropriate in a concluding chapter than in a preface. Just now, a preliminary
definition of the conservative idea is in order. (Kirk, *The
Conservative Mind*)[14]

A variation on this technique is to employ a metaphor:

The fox meets conflict undercover, while the lion prefers
the direct approach.

If your order follows a temporal sequence, years, days, or hours
provide natural transitions:

The following day the Helvetii struck camp and moved
out of the area. So did Caesar, who sent all his cavalry
ahead.... (Caesar, *Gallic War*, 1.16; trans. Hammond)

Or:

At length, in the beginning of May, with the help of
some of my acquaintances, rather to improve so good an
occasion for neighborliness than from any necessity, I
set up the frame of my house. (Henry David Thoreau,
Walden, "Economy")[15]

---

[13] C.S. Lewis, *The Four Loves* (Boston: Mariner Books, 2012), 106.
[14] Russell Kirk, *The Conservative Mind: From Burke to Eliot*, 7th ed. (Washington, DC: Regnery Books, 1987), 7.
[15] Henry David Thoreau, *Walden* (1854), ed. Lily Owens (New York: Arenel
Books, 1981), 49.

And, finally, the acronym:

> To lose weight, you must get SLIM: save calories, lose
> snacks, improve health, and make a resolution!

At the last paragraph

The conclusion fulfills the promise you made at the introduction.
Often, though not always, it should be your last paragraph. Here
is your final opportunity to impress your reader (or listener).
What to include? The classical handbook *Rhetorica ad Herennium*
(ca. 90 BC), suggests this template: "Conclusions . . . are tripartite,
consisting of the summing-up, amplification, and appeal to
pity."[16]

We can expand on each of these parts. Depending upon your
purpose, you might include from among the following: (1) *a
summary*: restate your thesis, enumerate your leading reasons;
(2) *an amplification*: draw an implication, drop a hook for what's
ahead; (3) *an appeal*: say what you want your audience to do,
warn them what will happen if they do not, set forth an example
of a person who did follow your advice. Once you have delivered
what you promised, stop writing. See which elements are present
in the following examples.

AN ACCEPTANCE SPEECH:
> In short, the book attempts a modest restatement of the
> Judeo-Christian notion that man is more than an organ-
> ism in an environment, more than an integrated person-
> ality, more even than a mature and creative individual,
> as the phrase goes. He is a wayfarer and a pilgrim.
>   I doubt that I succeeded, but I thank you for what you
> have done.
>   (Walker Percy on receiving National
>   Book Award for *The Moviegoer*, 1961)

---

[16] Cicero, *Rhetorica ad Herennium*, 2.30.47 (trans. Caplan). (Cicero's author-
ship of this work is disputed.)

A LETTER FROM JAIL:
I hope this letter finds you strong in the faith. I also hope that circumstances will soon make it possible for me to meet each of you, not as an integrationist or a civil-rights leader but as a fellow clergyman and a Christian brother. Let us all hope that the dark clouds of racial prejudice will soon pass away and the deep fog of mis-understanding will be lifted from our fear-drenched communities, and in some not too distant tomorrow the radiant stars of love and brotherhood will shine over our great nation with all their scintillating beauty.

Yours for the cause of Peace and Brotherhood.

> (Martin Luther King, Jr., *Letter from Birmingham Jail*, 1963)

A COMMENCEMENT ADDRESS:
If the world has not approached its end, it has reached a major watershed in history, equal in importance to the turn from the Middle Ages to the Renaissance. It will demand from us a spiritual blaze; we shall have to rise to a new height of vision, to a new level of life, where our physical nature will not be cursed, as in the Middle Ages, but even more importantly, our spiritual being will not be trampled upon, as in the Modern Era.

This ascension is similar to climbing onto the next anthropological stage. No one on earth has any other way left but—upward.

> (Alexander Solzhenitsyn, "A World Split Apart," at Harvard University, 1978)

To sum up, below is a diagram of the parts of the essay.

Schematic outline of the Essay
[Title]

In this essay I would like to explore [state question] _____.
This topic is interesting because [state value] _____.
In this essay I argue [state thesis]_____.
I will show this by first… second… third [state order]_____.

Subclaim 1: [repeat pattern below] _____.
Reason or argument in support of claim: _____.
Examples or illustrations: _____.

[Add hooks to lead into next topic sentence.]

In this essay I have argued:_____.
[restate your thesis and briefly tally main arguments]
One implication or corollary of the above is:_____.
[optional, though sometimes highly interesting]

VI

The Garden of Eloquence

*Practice traditional forms—Vary your speech—
Deploy literary figures*

19. Practice traditional forms

Imagine you discovered a cure for cancer, an instrument for looking through walls, and a new scientific language to boot! You'd not be far removed from the accomplishments of Sir Isaac Newton. How did he pull it off? It wasn't by trying to be creative. In a letter to Robert Hooke (dated February 5, 1676), who was himself an accomplished scientist, Newton explained his technique. With a remarkable humility, Newton confessed that if he'd seen farther than others it was only because he stood on the "shoulders of giants."

In this case what is true in the sciences is true in the arts. Innovation proceeds from tradition. To speak well, with clarity, and with credibility, imitate the masters. Read Cicero, study Churchill, listen to veteran preachers. In terms of the patterns of speech which you might employ, the formal structures you are likely to use, four stand out: the Pleasant Conversation, the Plain Speech, the Classical Sermon, and the Scholastic Dispute.

The Pleasant Conversation:
Or, The Fireside

Tell a story, draw a moral. Or, ask a question, and give an answer. This format draws the listener directly into conversation. It is simplest because it most nearly imitates casual speech. You begin with a tale or a problem, and then unravel it. If you have more to say, repeat the cycle. It works best for informal presentations. Its structure looks like this:

Q1	A1
Q2	A2
Q3	A3...

The Plain Style Speech:
Or, The Stroll

Here enters artifice. The Stroll is an essay performed. Simply state your Claim, give your Reason, illustrate with an Example, and re-state the Claim—CREC:

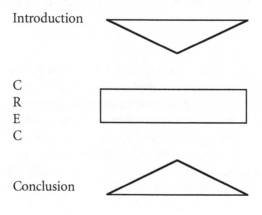

Introduction

C
R
E
C

Conclusion

The Classical Sermon:
Or, The Pitch

If you prefer to tell a story, or need to move your audience, choose this. The classical style builds upon the plain. It is more formal and, as such, more intellectually pleasing. Open your case (announce your subject, its value, your thesis); narrate (tell the story); supply your *confirmatio* (make your argument), and then your *peroratio* (conclusion).

There is, of course, great variety among sermons and orations. Still, if you follow the speech of an accomplished preacher or debater you will detect this skeleton. For examples you might start with Cicero's orations, or look to Augustine or Newman. Below is an ancient sermon for Holy Saturday, reprinted in the prayer book *The Liturgy of the Hours*.[1]

[OPENING/EXORDIUM]
Something strange is happening—there is a great silence on earth today, a great silence and stillness. The whole earth keeps silence because the King is asleep. The earth trembled and is still because God has fallen asleep in the flesh and he has raised up all who have slept ever since the world began. God has died in the flesh and hell trembles with fear.

[STORY/NARRATIO]
He has gone to search for our first parent, as for a lost sheep. Greatly desiring to visit those who live in darkness and in the shadow of death, he has gone to free from sorrow the captives Adam and Eve, he who is both God and the son of Eve. The Lord approached them bearing the cross, the weapon that had won him the victory. At the sight of him Adam, the first man he had created, struck his breast in terror and cried out to everyone: "My Lord be with you all." Christ answered him: "And with your spirit." He took him by the hand and raised him up, saying: "Awake, O sleeper, and rise from the dead, and Christ will give you light."

[ARGUMENT/CONFIRMATIO]
I am your God, who for your sake have become your son. Out of love for you and for your descendants I now by my own authority command all who are held in bondage to come forth, all who are in darkness to be enlightened, all who are sleeping to arise. I order you, O sleeper, to awake. I did not create you to be held a prisoner in hell.

---

[1] International Committee on English in the Liturgy, *The Liturgy of the Hours, Volume 2: Lenten Season and Easter Season* (New York: Catholic Book Publishing Company, 1976), 496–98.

Rise from the dead, for I am the life of the dead. Rise up, work of my hands, you who were created in my image. Rise, let us leave this place, for you are in me and I am in you; together we form only one person and we cannot be separated. For your sake I, your God, became your son; I, the Lord, took the form of a slave; I, whose home is above the heavens, descended to the earth and beneath the earth. For your sake, for the sake of man, I became like a man without help, free among the dead. For the sake of you, who left a garden, I was betrayed to the Jews in a garden, and I was crucified in a garden.

See on my face the spittle I received in order to restore to you the life I once breathed into you. See there the marks of the blows I received in order to refashion your warped nature in my image. On my back see the marks of the scourging I endured to remove the burden of sin that weighs upon your back. See my hands, nailed firmly to a tree, for you who once wickedly stretched out your hand to a tree.

I slept on the cross and a sword pierced my side for you who slept in paradise and brought forth Eve from your side. My side has healed the pain in yours. My sleep will rouse you from your sleep in hell. The sword that pierced me has sheathed the sword that was turned against you.

[CONCLUSION/PERORATIO]
Rise, let us leave this place. The enemy led you out of the earthly paradise. I will not restore you to that paradise, but I will enthrone you in heaven. I forbade you the tree that was only a symbol of life, but see, I who am life itself am now one with you. I appointed cherubim to guard you as slaves are guarded, but now I make them worship you as God. The throne formed by cherubim awaits you, its bearers swift and eager. The bridal chamber is adorned, the banquet is ready, the eternal dwelling places are prepared, the treasure houses of all good things lie open. The kingdom of heaven has been prepared for you from all eternity.

The Scholastic Dispute:
Or, The Duel

Developed in the medieval universities, the scholastic structure pursues truth through the clash of oppositions. You open with a question. Next, you consider the best objections and then cite an authority in your favor, followed by the positive reasons for your view. You end with a reply to the initial objections raised. Here is an example of a question taken from St. Thomas Aquinas's *Summa Theologica*. See how Thomas considers the question of whether man can ever lose his innate connection to moral truth. We'll analyze the features of his response below.

Whether the law of nature can
be abolished from the heart of man?

Objection 1. *It would seem that the natural law can be abolished from the heart of man. Because on Romans 2:14, "When the Gentiles who have not the law," etc. a gloss says that "the law of righteousness, which sin had blotted out, is graven on the heart of man when he is restored by grace." But the law of righteousness is the law of nature. Therefore the law of nature can be blotted out.*

Objection 2. *Further, the law of grace is more efficacious than the law of nature. But the law of grace is blotted out by sin. Much more therefore can the law of nature be blotted out.*

Objection 3. *Further, that which is established by law is made just. But many things are enacted by men, which are contrary to the law of nature. Therefore the law of nature can be abolished from the heart of man.*

On the contrary, *Augustine says (Confess. ii): "Thy law is written in the hearts of men, which iniquity itself effaces not." But the law which is written in men's hearts is the natural law. Therefore the natural law cannot be blotted out.*

I answer that, As stated above, there belong to the natural law, first, certain most general precepts, that are known to all; and secondly, certain secondary and more detailed precepts, which are, as it were, conclusions following closely from first principles. As to those general principles, the natural law, in the abstract, can nowise be blotted out from men's hearts. But it is blotted out in the case of a particular action, in so far as reason is hindered from applying the general principle to a particular point of practice, on account of concupiscence or some other passion, as stated above (Question 77, Article 2). But as to the other, i.e. the secondary precepts, the natural law can be blotted out from the human heart, either by evil persuasions, just as in speculative matters errors occur in respect of necessary conclusions; or by vicious customs and corrupt habits, as among some men, theft, and even unnatural vices, as the Apostle states (Romans 1), were not esteemed sinful.

Reply to Objection 1. Sin blots out the law of nature in particular cases, not universally, except perchance in regard to the secondary precepts of the natural law, in the way stated above.

Reply to Objection 2. Although grace is more efficacious than nature, yet nature is more essential to man, and therefore more enduring.

Reply to Objection 3. This argument is true of the secondary precepts of the natural law, against which some legislators have framed certain enactments which are unjust.

The virtues of a scholastic disputation are four. First, modesty. The disputation opens with a manageable question. Moderns are habitually immodest because impatient. St. Thomas asks not "Whether morals are relative," which is a big question, but whether the law of nature can be abolished from a man's heart. *Festina lente*—"hurry slowly"—was his motto. Questions are broken down into bite-sized baby chunks.

The second virtue: courtesy. Once he states the question he

gives you his opponents' best objections. Not only will he show you the alternatives, he'll even give a credible reason for why you might be tempted to believe in them. The third is piety. St. Thomas' *Summa* is studded with quotations—hundreds of them. He'll quote Scripture, of course, but also Aristotle, Plato, St. Augustine, St. Gregory, St. John Chrysostom, writers from the East, poets, and anyone with a shred of goodness. In culling from the past Thomas displays the virtue of devotion to one's ancestors; he takes the best, and tries to make it better. Finally, brevity. St. Thomas is clear, in part, because he is brief. He lunges for the essentials, and moves on. You can too.

20. Vary your speech

The aims, occasions, and subjects of your speech will vary. There is one rule, however, which remains: you must never bore. I suppose there are a hundred tricks funny people learn. Here's one even if you don't laugh like John Candy or look like Mr. Bean: *vary your speech*. The plague of boredom, observed Erasmus, can be avoided by someone "who has it at his fingertips to turn one idea into more shapes than Proteus himself is supposed to have turned into."[2]

Erasmus even offered a book of exercises to make the point. In his popular work on style, *Copia* (reprinted at least one hundred and sixty times between 1512 and 1600), he takes a sample sentence and reworks it. The sentence reads: "Your letter pleased me greatly." In the original, Erasmus reworks some 80-plus variations. Here's a short selection to get us started. To begin, notice the order of the words and their kind:

Your . . . . . . letter . . . . . pleased . . me . . . . greatly
[adjective] [noun]   [verb]   [pronoun] [adverb]

---

[2] Erasmus, *Copia: Foundations of the Abundant Style*, trans. and ed. B.I. Knott, in *Collected Works of Erasmus*, ed. C.R. Thompson, vol.24 (Toronto: University of Toronto Press, 1978), 302.

Now watch how he adds new color and texture to this basic shape. First, you might rearrange the order of the words:

> Your letter has delighted me very much.
> In a wonderful way your letter has delighted me.

Next, you could render an active voice passive:

> By your letter I have been greatly delighted.
> I have been delighted in an unusually wonderful way by your letter.

Then there are the beginnings and endings, the synonyms and the equivalent constructions:

> Your epistle has cheered me exceedingly.
> In truth by your epistle I have been exceedingly cheered.
> Your note has refreshed my spirit in no indifferent manner.

> From your most pleasing letter I have had incredible joy.
> Your paper has been the occasion of an unusual pleasure for me.

> From your paper I have received a wondrous pleasure.
> What you wrote has brought me the deepest delight.
> From what you wrote the deepest joy has been brought me.

> A by no means common joy has come to me from what you wrote.
> I have been uniquely delighted by your letter.
> How exceedingly your letter has delighted my spirit.

As the poet Gerard Manley Hopkins once wrote, "The world is charged with the grandeur of God." At its peak, art imitates nature. That grandeur is, perhaps, shown best in the details. Be sure to vary yours.

21. Deploy literary figures

The title for this chapter, *The Garden of Eloquence,* is lifted from Henry Peacham's 1577 Renaissance writer's manual. Though rhetoric is not widely studied today, from ancient Greece till about 1960 children were taught rhetoric's rudiments. This was done, largely, through the imitation of rhetorical figures, of memorable, pleasurable speech.

A figure, simply, is any unusual pattern of language employed for effect. Again we may cite Quintilian. He memorably defined a figure as "a form of speech artfully varied."[3] The use of figures does not guarantee good style. Thus, trite ideas trumpeted through brassy horns still grate. Indeed, they irritate all the more for their pomp. Rhyme and reason belong together. The tactful use of these devices, however, seems a humble pre-condition for good style. The intelligent disruption of the cadence of sounds and ideas can make a noble setting for worthwhile ideas. Variety pleases.

There is no set number of figures. The most commonly used rhetorical handbook throughout Medieval and Renaissance schools, *Rhetorica ad Herennium,* contained 65 figures. Peacham's Tudor guide contained 184. Farnsworth's recent *Classical English Rhetoric* builds off a list of 18. Below we illustrate ten.

A. Repetition & Word Play

Repetition—Reappearance for effect

> Ambition must be made to counteract ambition. The interest of the man must be connected with the constitutional rights of the place.
>
> (James Madison, *The Federalist* 51, 1788)

---

[3] "arte aliqua novata forma dicendi" (*Institutes,* 9.1.2).

Anaphora—Repetition at the start

> To-morrow, and to-morrow, and to-morrow/Creeps in
> this petty pace from day to day,/To the last syllable of
> recorded time;/And all our yesterdays have lighted fools/
> The way to dusty death.
>
> (Shakespeare, *Macbeth*, V.v.9–23)

> And so, too, as regards this world, with all its enjoy-
> ments, yet disappointments. Let us not trust it; let us not
> give our hearts to it; let us not begin with it. Let us begin
> with faith; let us begin with Christ. . . .
>
> (Newman, *Parochial and Plain Sermons*, "The Cross
> of Christ, Measure of the World," conclusion)

Alliteration—Repetition of sound

> Already American vessels had been searched, seized, and
> sunk. Tales of atrocities to our seamen filled the press.
>
> (John F. Kennedy, *Profiles in Courage*, 1961)

Epistrophe—Repetition at the end

> When I was a child, I spoke like a child, I thought like a
> child, I reasoned like a child; when I became a man, I
> gave up childish ways.   (1 Corinthians 13:11, RSV)

> Faustus: And what are you that live with Lucifer?
> Mephistophilis: Unhappy spirits that fell with Lucifer,/
> Conspir'd against our God with Lucifer,/And are for
> ever damn'd with Lucifer.
>
> (Marlowe, *Dr. Faustus*, scene iii.)

> I'll have my bond! Speak not against my bond!/I have
> sworn an oath that I will have my bond!
>
> (Shakespeare, *The Merchant of Venice*, III.iii.3–4)

That perfect liberty they sigh for—the liberty of making slaves of other people—Jefferson never thought of; their own father never thought of; they never thought of themselves, a year ago.

(Lincoln, debate with Stephen Douglas at Peoria, 1854)

B. Structural Devices

Parallel structure

Publicly I was a teacher of the arts which they call liberal; privately I professed a false religion—in the former role arrogant, in the latter superstitious, in everything vain.   (St. Augustine, *Confessions*, 4.1; trans. Chadwick)

The mother looked young, and the daughter looked old; the mother's complexion was pink, and the daughter's was yellow; the mother set up for frivolity, and the daughter for theology.

(Dickens, *Great Expectations*, 1861)

The aim of the sculptor is to convince us that he is a sculptor; the aim of the orator is to convince us that he is not an orator.   (G. K. Chesterton, *Heretics*, 1905)

You must make your choice. Either this man was, and is, the Son of God, or else a madman or something worse. You can shut him up for a fool, you can spit at him and kill him as a demon or you can fall at his feet and call him Lord and God, but let us not come with any patronizing nonsense about his being a great human teacher.

(C. S. Lewis, *Mere Christianity*, 1952)

Likewise, when [democratic values] are threatened anywhere, they are threatened everywhere.

(Canadian Prime Minister Stephen Harper, *Address to the Israeli Parliament*, 2014)

Antithesis—Juxtaposition of ideas

> When I am frightened by what I am to you, then I am
> consoled by what I am with you. For to you I am the
> bishop, with you I am a Christian. The first names an
> office, the second a grace; the first a danger, the second,
> salvation.   (St. Augustine, *Sermon* 340.1)

> What then can be the reason why we lament more him
> that dies of a wound than that dies of a fever? A Man
> that languishes with disease, ends his life with more
> pain, but with less virtue, he leaves no example to his
> friends, nor bequeaths any honour to his descendants.
>   (Samuel Johnson, Letter to Bennet Langton,
>   September 1758)

> Those who have been left out, we will try to bring in.
> Those left behind, we will help to catch up.
>   (Richard Nixon, *Inaugural Address*, 1969)

Chiasmus—Reversal

> When the going gets tough, the tough get going!

> Ask not what your country can do for you, but what you
> can do for your country.

> We shape our buildings, and afterwards our buildings
> shape us.
>   (Churchill, Speech in the House of Commons, 1943)

> It may be true that the law can't change the heart, but it
> can restrain the heartless. It may be true that the law
> can't make a man love me, but it can restrain him from
> lynching me, and I think that's pretty important also.
>   (Martin Luther King, Jr., Address to
>   Ohio Northern University, 1968)

C. Dramatic Touches

Adage—Memorable proverb

> Tempus fugit! (*Time flies!*)
> Gloria mundi transit. (*The glory of the world passes.*)
> Quis custodiet ipsos custodies? (*Who will guard the guards themselves?*)
>
> A bird in the bag is better than two in the bush!
> Man proposes; God disposes.
> If you want peace, seek justice.
> Two wrongs don't make a right!
> You are not a dollar bill that everyone should like you.

Simile—Comparison

> He giveth snow like wool: he scattereth the hoarfrost like ashes. He casteth forth his ice like morsels: who can stand before his cold? (Psalm 147:16–17, KJV)
>
> From the hill beyond the fort, it looked like a little doll house sitting on the edge of a great big table, with a brown tablecloth smoothed out flat all around it.
> (Ralph Moody, *Little Britches: Father and I Were Ranchers*, 1950)
>
> The sentences [of Voltaire] frisk past like little goblins, with eyes as bright as fire; as lively today as the day they were born. (F.L. Lucas, *Style*, 1955)

Metaphor—Compressed comparison

> All embarked, the party launched out on the sea's foaming lanes while the son of Atreus told his troops to wash. . . . (Homer, *Iliad*, 1:365–367; trans. Fagles)

I came to Carthage and all around me hissed a cauldron
of illicit loves.

> (St. Augustine, *Confessions*, 3.1; trans. Chadwick)

Conscience is a coward. Those faults which it has not
courage enough to prevent it seldom has justice enough
to accuse.

> (Oliver Goldsmith, *The Vicar of Wakefield*, 1766)

VII

First Thoughts and Last

Write at the beginning—Attend to disposition and delivery—
Review intelligently—Nihil nimius—Wed truth to beauty

22. Write at the beginning

Having considered the three means of persuasion, the aims, and
the elements of speech, we've gathered all the pieces of the puz-
zle. Now we set them together. It is time to consider the process
of composition itself.

How to prepare for a speech? You have several mechanisms
at your disposal, ranging from the less to the more elaborate.
Least intrusive of all is to walk through a checklist. Before rising,
you may mentally enumerate the two or three ideas you wish to
communicate, and then deliver them. This is fine for short talks,
or informal replies. In most cases, however, you will need to plan
in advance. This means you will need to write.

There is a common prejudice among young speakers that it
is better to speak off the cuff than to speak off the page. Usually
this is not the case. Preparation does not stifle authenticity.
Authenticity, like "creativity," is a studied art. As Michelangelo
once counseled, you must take "infinite pains" if you are "to
make something that looks effortless."[1] The reason? You were not
born whole. You will act or speak with authenticity only after a
long study of nature, beginning with your own. In the meantime,
you must practice. And that means work.

J.K. Rowling, mother of the *Harry Potter* series, was once
asked how she prepares to write her books. She replied this way:

[1] Cited in Lukas' *Style*, 242.

I do a plan. I plan, I really plan quite meticulously. I
know it is sometimes quite boring because when people
say to me, "I write stories at school and what advice
would you give me to make my stories better?" And I
always say—and people's face often fall when I say—
"You have to plan," and they say "Oh, I prefer just writing and seeing where it takes me." Sometimes writing
and seeing where it takes you will lead you to some really
good ideas but I would say nearly always it won't be as
good as if you sat down first and thought: Where do I
want to go, what end am I working towards, what would
be good, a good start? Sorry, very dull.

Dull, but true.

When you begin as a speaker, write your speech in its
entirety. This gives you the opportunity to improve your grasp of
the formal devices (parallel structure, word choice, etc.) of persuasive speech. When it comes time to deliver the text, you might
or might not follow the script exactly. Still, the repeated exercise
of writing before delivering will build your skills. And it saves
time. As Quintilian observed, it is best to "conduct one's work
from start to finish in such a way that it will need merely to be
chiseled, not wholly recast."[2]

Sometimes people think that informal speeches don't
require preparation. That is a mistake. In fact, they often require
more work. The less time you have to make your point, the more
precise you need to be. In light of this, bring notes at first. Silly
and entertaining talks benefit from this discipline as much as do
formal presentations.

Nolens volens, willingly or unwillingly, you may be asked to
give a toast. Even old pros follow this advice. I was once at a formal dinner where a professor from Cambridge University
famous for his wit gave a hilarious, apparently off-the-cuff after-

---

[2] *Institutes*, 10.3.17.

dinner speech. His delivery was natural. His jokes were well-timed. Word-plays, the sequence of stories, the lessons drawn: each was subtly crafted. Was I witnessing the spontaneous effervescence of genius? Well, yes and no. He shuffled his notes. I saw his cue cards. Eventually, such prompts become less necessary; at the beginning, though, and even at the middle of your career, before you speak, write.

23. Attend to disposition and delivery

The day of your presentation has arrived. Remember to sing your scale. Then, consider your disposition and delivery. We'll note a few other details along the way.

Before you arrive, clarify your *disposition*. You can do this by reviewing a few basic questions. What do you wish to accomplish? Do you wish to teach (what?), please (how?), move (where?)? Recall again the points of the communication triangle. What is your role in the event (are you the teacher, the student, the pilgrim, the boss, the friend?)? Your position at the event will help you to judge your obligations accurately. Some people think that assertiveness is the cardinal sin among managers. Others seem to prize decisiveness above all else. These are both half-truths.

To judge your disposition you must look not to abstract principle, but to context. An authoritarian manner is usually odious, but the exercise of authority isn't. For example, if you are chairing a meeting, and a contentious matter arises, by all means collect opinions. This is a sign not of weakness but of courtesy. It gives you the opportunity to be moved by contrary views without being contrarian. As king Solomon said, "A gentle answer turns away wrath." Still, once the time comes to render a decision, pray and act. If a decision cannot be achieved, table it, and set a time when you will return.

Consider also your *delivery*. Do not mumble. You likely have certain verbal tics. Students of mine have found the following advice useful. Two days before their presentation, I encourage students to sit a friend in front of them as a "mock" audience. Each time they say "ah" or "um" or add a distracting filler, they are to have their friend ring a bell. They feel embarrassed. But they improve; so will you.

Moving forward, you've now arrived at the event. What's next? Having prepared inwardly, you must now turn to externals. It's best to arrive early, and expect to reflect long. Both immediately before and after your talk there is work to do.

Be punctual. You do not have to be the first in the room, but you cannot be the last. I was once giving a public lecture, and rushed in late from a class I had been teaching. One of the organizers tried to console me by saying, "don't worry, nothing can start without you!" A kind sentiment, but one you should not adopt. In business, an accepted rule of thumb is to be ready ten minutes before your appointment. Good reasons support this habit. Though the organizers are responsible for the material layout of the event, ask yourself: if things go badly, is it your fault or theirs?

Always consider the fault to be yours (barring riots). If something is amiss, correct it. After a few years of practice, you will have more experience than most organizers. When you arrive, scan the room. Is there water at the podium? Is the lighting as you would wish? (The more light on you, the better.) Has the microphone been checked? If not, tap, tap. Is your watch handy? Are chairs in the correct order?

Seating deserves attention. When you speak, any large gap which separates you from your listeners will drain away your energy, and theirs. If a gulf separates the right lung of the room from the left, have someone slide an extra chair from the end of every row into the middle so as to narrow the gap. You came to speak to people, not to pavement. If the group fits well in a quarter of the space, cluster. Also, avoid what I like to think of as the "dead man's divide." Moses crossed the Red Sea, but your voice will not. Prefer to speak no longer than two arms' length from the person seated in front of you. It matters less how many rows deep the auditorium goes than the distance between yourself and the first row.

Professional speakers attest that the nearer you are to your audience, the stronger your emotional connection will be. If you can reach out to the first person (see if you could grab their arm), the man in the back row will feel a little as though you could also touch his. I am not sure why this effect occurs. But it does occur. Sporting events offer an obvious analogy. Imagine you shared Fenway Park between yourself and the hot-dog seller. You would likely save your voice. Add a few thousand bodies, and every hit draws forth a yell. We are social. Even if the individuals at your talk have little in common, once they enter the room they will quickly assume a collective identity. Do not neglect this advantage. Place yourself near to your audience.

I am always happy to ask people to shift seats. I recall one talk where a friend of mine had set up a speaking engagement at a large church in a city where I had never been. The organizer knew nothing of me, and had no idea how many people might attend (20… 200?). I showed up. So did five or six others. Luckily for us, the five who did come happened to belong to the catering club in the parish. Before and after the talk we enjoyed a feast fit for a Boy Scout brigade!

This sort of thing can be embarrassing for the planner, and it might be for you. Oh well, take comfort. As Mother Teresa once observed, "We learn humility through accepting humiliations." The goal of learning rhetoric is not better to serve yourself, but to train yourself better to serve others. As you can imagine, the few lonely souls who wandered into the church for my presentation scattered themselves like sea gulls across an empty beach, waiting to see what might happen next. I asked everyone to join me in the front. The event was intimate, but mostly enjoyable. I still offered a lecture. I asked questions, and our small size allowed for debate. The point is: adapt the space to your numbers. You came, after all, to speak to people, not to pews.

So much for the physical plan of the room. Just as important is the emotional territory into which you have entered. Arriving early lets you draw a rough sketch of the characters before whom you are about to stand. How do they feel: Happy? Hostile? Haggard? What is the demographic? A younger audience will both give and require more energy (usually) than an older one.

University chaplaincies across North America host events called "Theology on Tap." The aim of the event is to con some hapless professor into joining a group of rowdy students at a pub to talk about God so that he can be heckled by anyone who happens to be holding a beer that night. I know someone who was to serve as the "theologian" on tap one evening. His topic: "Is the pope always right?" This chap rarely shows up at pubs. After he shuffled through the doors of the jolly old *James Joyce* he realized the night was going to be loud, and contemplated a quick exit. When you find yourself in the middle of a jungle you must come to a clear decision: either take your stand or dash out the back. He fortified his shaking knees with hops. The students were loud. Most of us had fun. The owners told us never to return. Know your audience.

Of course, not every group is waiting for a party. At more formal events, you will often find yourself in the midst of a line-up of speakers. Here is another reason to arrive early. Your presence allows you to pick up on what was said before you open your mouth. Sometimes you can piggy-back on another's idea. If you do, be moderate. At conferences it is tiring if speaker number four defers to speaker number three who deferred to speakers number two and one. Presumably, you came with ideas. Present them. If what someone else has said can help you make your point better, draw from them, possibly even to draw a contrast; if not, let it lie.

A last reason to arrive early: it shows courtesy. The organizer has a dozen problems to contend with. Subtract one of them by your presence.

24. Review intelligently
You've planned and executed your talk; what's left? Every high school football coach knows that preparation does not end with

the game. It ends with the tapes. Preparation for your next talk begins with review of this talk.

It need not be onerous. A few lines in a notebook scribbled while the sweat still wets your brow will lodge the essentials in your head. Record both the memorable and the forgettable. Cologne Cathedral wasn't perfected in a day, and neither will your speech be. Here is a list of questions you might wish to ask immediately after your talk or presentation:

- Did I act in accord with my end?
- Did I accurately read the audience?
- Did I anticipate and reply to questions?
- Did I avoid fillers?
- Did I keep control of my emotions?

G.K. Chesterton said once that anything worth doing is worth doing badly. Words to live by. You could not anticipate what happened, you say? See if you can't salvage a draw from a disaster. A few stories come to mind.

I am still waiting for the chance to be shouted out of a room, but I do vividly remember the first time I gave a radio interview. I had written a book. I was to be questioned on its themes. I had prepared for a week. My office was plastered with flow-charts and quotations, facts, and figures of speech. Not wishing to disappoint the millions of eager, attentive radio-listening commuters who would be barreling down the nation's interstates that afternoon (so I imagined), I was ready for the show! The phone rang.

I soon discovered two facts which I could not alter. First: the station was in the midst of a national pledge-drive. My segment was to be compressed to make room for a heart-rendering story about a miracle-baby which some saintly parents from Ohio had rescued. Second: the interviewer knew nothing of my book. After the introductions and a few pleasantries he asked: "So, what were the Guilds like in the Middle Ages?" Guilds? How was I to know? I knew as much about Medieval Guilds as about the mating habits of Canadian geese. And then it was over. Certainly, the experience extinguished any subconscious ambitions I may have nursed to become an anchor at CNN or Fox News. Expect problems, but don't dwell on them. Prepare, review, give thanks, and move on.

Of course, not all problems are so politely resolved. Public universities are not quite what they used to be. It was the radical Voltaire who once said, "I may disagree with what you say, but I will defend to the death your right to say it." His great-grandchildren often disappoint. Today, if your speech offends, prepare for a disturbance. Sometimes, you can banter. I once attended a talk by a senior politician who was traveling across the country speaking on energy and foreign policy. The hippie protesters took their seats. Each time the poor man said "oil" the collective shouted back something like "blood." The politician carried on. To the annoyance of many, so did the protesters. When the shouting increased, he occasionally addressed the group with brief comments, and then returned to his text. Questions came and went. The crowd dispersed. The hippies rode home.

Copy his example. If you can, incorporate the hecklers... a little. Mostly you should ignore them, but some back and forth can re-establish your authority, and even give you a chance to discredit their claims, if you must. Disruptions are nothing new. Ancient Greeks had to manage them. In his public-speaking manual written for Alexander the Great, Aristotle suggested that, when an uproar arises, you ought to throw back an adage or maxim. At first, you might try to answer their objections with a phrase like this: "I too would like us to have more green energy. But, while we work on the technology, we still need secure oil." Contain the protest as long as you can.

If banter will not work, and it's clear the ship is sinking, go down with gusto. A talk that is out of hand is like a house that has caught on fire. The house may well go up in flames, but rest assured the neighborhood is watching. All eyes stay fixed on you. As the speaker, you thus retain advantages, even if you are shouted down. The emotion of the audience will follow your response.

Don't stand idle. You must either advance or retreat. Use the microphone while you can. Once banter becomes useless, address the audience. More often than not the room will be filled with as many of "us" as "them." You might say something like, "We respect these folks' right to disagree, but we would also like them to respect our right to meet peacefully." Spontaneous clapping might ensue, if you are lucky, maybe even enough to discourage the rowdies. If not, try to discredit the protesters and clearly call for help: "I don't see why a few extremists should stop the rest of us from having a rational conversation. Why don't the rest of you who would like to continue this gathering clap loudly to let these folks know the rest of us would like them to keep quiet!" If you have friends, they will clap. If members of the crowd start pushing, publicly ask the security to step in.

A little bit of indignation on your part can actually calm a tense situation. An incident I witnessed at a rodeo not long ago comes to mind. Ah, the joys of cowboy life! Now, if you've ever spent time around real cowboys, men and women who've been riding since they were walking, you've witnessed up close something of that devoted affection that is neither sentimental nor merely utilitarian. When it comes to animals, city folks tend to slouch toward extremes. Cowboys hit the mean. Well, in the midst of the afternoon's festivities—we had just finished the calf-wrangling, if memory serves—plop! It was as if an army of angry beetles had swarmed into the ring. They yelped. They flopped dead. The rodeo halted. The protesters had arrived.

Poor souls. It appears they had driven in from the big city, Vancouver, I think. Shouts to the effect of "Let freedom reign!" or "Stop the cruelty!" rang across the dusty ring. My point is not to discuss what happens to a young brain on Peter-Singer-juice.[3] I

---

[3] Definition: 1. Peter Singer: utilitarian philosopher who famously advocates that some pets are worth more than some children, and that victims of dementia ought to be euthanized to save money (though when his own mother got Alzheimer's he claimed her situation was "different"); 2. Peter-Singer-Juice:

want to highlight how the cool of the Master of Ceremonies saved a few thoughtless kids from getting their hides tanned.

The crowd would've loved a lynching. Who were these kids anyway, lecturing country folk? Likely they'd never changed a dirty kitty litter, let alone spent an afternoon on a working farm. Over my shoulder, all throughout the fiasco, a man kept yelling "Rope 'em! Rope 'em!" I confess I wish I had brought mine. But the man with the mic kept his cool. He calmly denounced the young intruders, pointing out that no one in this ring was for cruelty, and how well the cowboys and gals cared for their animals. The MC's moderate indignation soothed the protesters. His good mind turned a poor showing into a humorous interruption.

One last story comes to mind. Recently, a pro-life member of the Canadian parliament gave a lecture at a university campus in Ontario. Or, I should say, he tried to. A few minutes into his talk, a man dressed in a costume mimicking the female reproductive organ began yelling obscenities while accomplices seized the microphone. The member of Parliament asked security to intervene. They declined. And so, the speaker quietly packed up his suitcase and prepared to leave. Within hours images zipped around the internet. He lost the event, but his cause won credibility.

I suppose it's what marks a professional. When the party heats up, rest assured that someone will begin recording the event; so have fun, but maintain self-possession. If the disturbance continues and you know you are on the way out, you may wish to throw out ironic statements: "I thought this university believed in free speech!," or the like. At other times, a silent retreat is best. Cultivate prudence, and study professionals. You will learn as much from others' mistakes as your own.

The easy consumption of utilitarian thinking (e.g., that the strong are better than the weak) without digesting the consequences.

25. *Nihil nimius*

"The only difficulty was that though the universe had been disposed of, I myself was left over." A marvelous line from Walker Percy's *The Moviegoer*. After you've grasped all the rules, what's left? You are. What remains is that you develop a habit for composition. This is no easy task. My best advice is to echo an ancient proverb: *nihil nimius*, nothing too much.

My last counsel has nothing to do with writing or speaking, but rather with living. Constructing a productive routine is evidently a question of practical psychology. There are, perhaps, as many ways of writing as there are writers. Stendhal preferred to dictate, whereas Milton had it forced upon him in old age. Wordsworth apparently wrote while walking or in bed; Trollope glued himself to the desk for timed sessions (250 words per quarter hour). Chesterton never read twice what he wrote, while Montaigne never stopped editing, even after his manuscript saw print. The place, the time, the circumstances seem to vary so greatly across temperaments and oceans that one may begin to feel that every man is to be left merely to his own devices.

This seems to me an unnecessary concession. In my experience most young writers will find themselves occupying one of two camps. Call them the "romantics" and the "reliables." The romantics write in a fevered pitch of excitement, after sporadic starts, and for long durations. The reliables keep to a schedule. The romantics dream of constructing the ideal paper; the reliables deliver essays to their professor on time. The romantic spurns the waking hours to stalk the virgin night in search of fruitful inspiration. The reliable books an appointment with the muses, and expects them to keep it.

In truth, each has a stake to claim. Writing is neither a wholly deliberate nor a wholly inspired activity. Each of us, now and again, will be favored with a bright idea. The trick is to keep them from scuffling off, like mischievous mice, back into their black holes.

I think a writer ought never to be far from pen and paper. He ought at any hour to be prepared to welcome what manna might befall him. And yet, on the whole, the morsels have a better hope of being gathered into a meal if you make a habit of expecting them. If you are a musician or play a sport you have ready access to this secret. Fifteen minutes a day banging at the piano keys is far more productive, in the long run, than sporadic two-hour practice sessions. So too with writing. Make it a habit.

Studies suggest the same. I have at hand a report of research on two groups of young professors. Both had obligations to write. Both groups, roughly corresponding to "romantics" and "reliables," had strong views about their approach to their task. The results are worth pondering. After a two-year period of observation, in every respect the reliables were more productive, happier, and left with more time for service and friendships than were the romantics.

The results may startle, but they are understandable. You are more than your work. If your life is off-balance, if you do not pay your respects to sleep, to play, to prayer, then your writing, like everything else, is bound to unravel. *Nothing too much.*

26. Wed truth to beauty

I conclude with a confession. At the end of my undergraduate career, when I was a student at a university on the Canadian prairies, I began attending an Anglican church. The preacher was a celebrity. Students, believing or not, would flock to his little parish. They may have wandered in for the music, but they stayed for the preacher. He was a good man, to be sure. But it was his words which enticed. By some alchemy, which I've never yet seen repeated, he was able to transform the rough and sharp ideas of a Dostoevsky, of a Donne, of St. Paul, into a shimmering display, spinning, as it were, what first appeared as lifeless straw into shimmering gold. I finished my studies, moved off with my new bride to England, and left the parish but not the preacher.

Moderns maintain a peculiar relationship with rhetoric. We no longer teach it to our young, nor demand it of our wise. What since ancient Athens was considered an essential skill for a free citizen has now largely been consigned to hucksters and to the tarmacs of used car dealerships. The tragedy is that we abandoned the art on purpose. About the same time the Russians flung Sputnik into space, in the name of progress American, Canadian, and British educators tossed the old grammar and style books onto the intergalactic rubbish heap of history.

The past was trashed. In a scientific age, so the reasoning went, questions of philosophy, of beauty, of sex, of God, could be set aside in favor of technological solutions. The science was settled. Just the same, the timing couldn't have been worse. Who would've foreseen that at the same hour the West turned its back on its humanistic traditions, it would be called to police the global order, shore up markets, and shoot down terrorists?

In a way, the educational experiments of the 1970s already look quaint. Of course the project was doomed. The fruits of self-expression without discipline, of creativity without culture, were bound to disappoint. And they have. The problem was that few at the time seemed to notice that while success in space lent prestige to the sciences, back here on earth, the public school-factories were genetically re-modifying our most precious national commodity: our kids. The average child these days slumps in front of a television about 25 hours a week. That's not counting face-to-Facebook time. Never mind untangling split infinitives. Fed for 12 years on self-esteem happy juice, and left to their own devices, a hefty minority (about 13%, actually) of American high school grads today can no longer read well enough to fill out a McDonald's job application.

Well, this at least is how I've heard grumpy professors speak. Perhaps the past is past. One thing is clear. In education, nearly everyone agrees that ours is a time of reconstruction, that we must grow in goodness or perish. A nation run by technical giants but ethical dwarves is hardly a nation worth defending. Such a land, marred as it will be by slovenly speech and vapid slogans, will decay into an ugly dwelling, because it will be ruled by Orcs.

Since ancient times, the fundamental problem of politics has been this: How to reconcile wisdom and power? Or, in an updated idiom: How can we preserve man from his own destructive technologies? How can we ennoble freedom, and rescue ourselves from a post-human future? This is where rhetoric, wedded to philosophy and faith, can offer a modest contribution.

After my sojourn at Oxford, I returned to Canada, and then to the US, as a professor. While I myself am neither a politician nor a cleric, I never forgot that preacher. Most of all I never forgot the lesson that he taught by his example. What he offered to us young souls was the hope that, even in this world, truth might marry beauty. It is a lesson the good can be tempted to forget. I trust it is a lesson we can learn better to defend.

Appendix:
Study Guide

Most skills are learned best by imitation. This is certainly true of persuasive writing and speech. For those zealous readers who not only like knowing the 26 rules but wish to practice applying them, I offer these tools. Included is a list of the rules; a sequence of imitative exercises based on each chapter; and, finally, titles of poems that could be profitably memorized.

The Rules

1. Master grammar
2. Observe three precepts
3. Learn a little Logic
4. Avoid fallacies
5. Embody *Proportio*
6. Move head and heart
7. Use vivid language
8. Prefer the concrete
9. Cultivate the virtues
10. Don't overstate
11. Speak with your body
12. Move with your motions
13. Muster your voice
14. Begin from ends

15. Match means to ends
16. Perfect the essay
17. Open with a hook
18. Mark transitions
19. Practice traditional forms
20. Vary your speech
21. Deploy literary figures
22. Write at the beginning
23. Attend to disposition and delivery
24. Review intelligently
25. *Nihil nimius*
26. Wed truth to beauty

The Exercises

I
Logos: **Rational Speech**

1. Master grammar
Clarity is your first obligation.
Grammar is the precondition of clarity.

1.1. Read again Lewis Carroll's pun. Imitating his structure, offer two of your own.
1.2. "A woman, without her man, is nothing...." Use this as a model to come up with two more humorous couplets.
1.3. Grab a grammar. What is the proper use of a semicolon?

2. Observe three precepts
Omit needless words. Use the
active voice. Use parallel structure.

2.1. Following the pattern offered, come up with your own list of wordy sentences whose first words could be reduced to the following: He...; Since...; Although...; Likely...; Her mother likes....
2.2. On the model of the transformation of "He was hit by the ball" into "The ball hit him," generate four sentences in the passive voice; then reduce them to the active.
2.3. One of the most memorable passages from the New Testament is Christ's Sermon on the Mount (esp. Mt. 5:3–11). Imitating the style, write a series of commendations for a model husband or wife.

3. Learn a little logic
Logic is the language of God. Learn the three acts of the mind.
Distinguish truth from validity, the probable from the certain.

3.1. Define "understanding." Offer three examples of "terms."
3.2. Define "judging." Offer three examples of "propositions."
3.3. Write a valid syllogism with a false conclusion. Then write an invalid syllogism with a true conclusion.

4. Avoid six fallacies
Fallacies are arguments that merely appear valid.
Avoid mistakes of understanding, judging, and reasoning.

4.1. On amphiboly and equivocation: "The manager reserves the right to exclude any man or woman they consider proper." Compose two other statements that could also be misconstrued.
4.2. On false cause and *post hoc ergo propter hoc*: "The cock crows, the sun rises...." Offer two additional problematic claims that likewise mistake correlation for causation.
4.3. Logically, what's the problem with an *ad hominem*? Identify a situation when someone's character would be relevant to consider.

II
Pathos: **Proportionate emotion**

5. Embody *Proportio*
Proportio manifests character.
Make your emotions correspond to
the context. Don't look like an elephant in a dress.

5.1. Define *proportio*. Describe an action that manifests *proportio*. Cite two that would not.
5.2. Why does a skyscraper not evoke the same feeling as a mountain?
5.3. Name and describe a person you know directly whom you regard as manifesting *proportio*.

6. Move head and heart
Appeal to reason and emotion.

6.1. What led to Demosthenes's eventual success in the courts?
6.2. Recount a time you were convinced by someone's speech, but repulsed by their manner of saying it.
6.3. Recite to a partner the passage from Plutarch that reads "…being convinced how much grace and ornament…" once with proportionate emotion, and a second time with disproportionate emotion.

7. Use vivid language
Vivid language brings clarity and delight.

7.1. Following the style and structure of Mowat's account of the Canadian prairie, write a description of a prairie storm in your own words. Then, using the same template, write a description of a tropical storm or a January blizzard.

8. Prefer the concrete
Vivid language is concrete. Pathos aims at delight.

8.1. Using Erasmus' sketch as a model, in two or three paragraphs, describe a friend, relation, or leader whom you admire.

III
Ethos: Credible Character

9. Cultivate the virtues
"Style is character embodied in speech" (F. L. Lucas).
"The orator is a good man, eloquent in speech" (Quintilian).
All lesser and greater virtues relate to the four cardinal virtues.

9.1. Why does the notion of character imply belief in free will?
9.2. Why is the counsel "Be natural!" less than sufficient?

9.3. Chart the correspondence between the three parts of the soul and the four cardinal virtues.

10. Don't overstate
Distinguish between certain, probable,
and doubtful claims. "The madman has lost
everything but his reason" (G.K. Chesterton).

10.1. Why are our judgments of the causes for changes in surface sea temperatures (SST) at best probable?

10.2. Why do we expect more certainty from a problem in mathematics than from a judgment about someone's character?

10.3. Recount an occasion when a speaker lost credibility in your eyes because of a rash judgment.

11. Speak with your body
You project ethos through words and motions.
"Only a shallow person does not judge by appearances"
(Oscar Wilde).

11.1. Recount a time a speaker was under-dressed.

11.2. Name the 3 "V's." What is helpful about Mehrabian's research? What are its limits?

12. Move with your motions
Master the three types of motions: change of position,
change of motion, and change of tempo. "Once I saw it
I suspected he was lying" (FBI Agent).

12.1. Read to a friend the passage from Doyle ("By a man's finger nails...") once flat, without any movement; then a second time with your eyes above their head; and finally a third time with your eyes shifting quickly. What do these motions convey?

13. Muster your voice
Any voice can improve.
Any alteration from an expected tempo, pitch,
or projection will convey a distinct meaning.

13.1 Practice singing the scale.

13.2. Do it again the next three mornings after rising from sleep. See if you'd like to make it a habit.

13.3. Read again Doyle's passage (from 12.1) and see if by your voice you can render the text "spooky"; try a second time to make it humorous.

IV
The Aims of the Speaker

14. Begin from ends
Your immediate aim is either to teach, to please, or to move. To teach, be clear; to please, be vivid; to move, make direct appeal.

14.1. Imagine a friend has asked you to submit a 300-word essay, for their private reflection only, on "whether war is sometimes necessary." Your aim is to teach. Write that essay.

14.2. Now imagine this same friend is about to join the Marines. He is, however, undecided on the question of whether war is ever licit. Your aim is to move. Re-write the original essay.

15. Match means to ends
Learn the communication triangle.
Oratory may be on a small, medium or grand scale.

15.1. Explain the function of each point on the triangle.

15.2. Recount a time when someone's speech moved you to action. Recount another time when someone's speech did not move you. With reference to the points on the triangle, name the differences between the two situations.

V
The Elements of a Speech

16. Perfect the essay
The essay is a literary device for saying "almost everything about almost anything" (Aldous Huxley). "When eloquence draws attention to itself it does wrong by the substance of things" (Montaigne).

16.1. Grab a past essay you've written, or write now a 400-word essay on the question "What is the correct definition of evil?" Or, if you prefer, "What would be the perfect summer holiday?"

16.2. Now, mark in red your introduction, body, conclusion, and any transition sentences (in the essay from 16.1).

17. Open with a hook
Your introduction need not be creative.
Use hook, line, and sinker.

17.1. Following the examples of hooks supplied, compose two more. Using your own model essay, identify yours, or add one now.

17.2. Did your essay contain a one-line thesis or statement of purpose? If not, make it clear.

17.3. If your essay did not include a statement of structure (sinker), add one.

18. Mark transitions
The body of your paper is a whole divided into logical parts. Transitions mark these parts. Conclusions include the summing-up, an amplification, and an appeal to pity
(Rhetorica ad Herennium).

18.1. Pick two types of transition statements. Adapt and insert these into your essay.

18.2. Study the three model conclusions given. Following the same structure, re-write one of these in your own words.

18.3. Now, given the above, re-write the conclusion to your own essay.

VI
The Garden of Eloquence

19. Practice traditional forms
*Innovation proceeds from tradition. "If I have seen farther
it is because I stood on the shoulders of giants" (Sir Isaac Newton).
Imitate four forms.*

19.1. Take up your essay on "the correct definition of evil" (or your own earlier essay) and recast it into the form of a fireside chat.
19.2. Render it this time into an oration.
19.3. Finally, try the scholastic article.

20. Vary your speech
*Practice common literary devices. "Boredom can be avoided by
someone who can turn an idea into more shapes than Proteus"
(Erasmus).*

20.1. Study Erasmus' models. Take the sentence "His painting pleased me greatly" and offer ten variations.

21. Deploy literary figures
*Unite rhyme and reason.
"A figure is a form of speech artfully deployed"
(Quintilian).*

21.1. Memorize two passages from the list of quotations.
21.2. With Madison's repetition as a model, come up with two similar sentences of your own.
21.3. Do the same for Kennedy's alliteration.
21.4. Using Charles Dickens' passage, contrast a plumber and a painter.
21.5. With an eye to the adages given, compose three of your own.

VII
First Thoughts and Last

22. Write at the beginning
Authenticity is a studied art.
"I plan, I really plan quite meticulously"
(J.K. Rowling).

22.1. What are arguments for and against writing out a speech (say, of ten minutes in length) prior to its delivery?

22.2. For your next essay, speech, or sermon, draft a one-page outline. If you have none forthcoming, draft a one-page outline for the following topic: "Whether music, irrespective of lyrics, can communicate a moral message."

22.3. Imagine your brother has just graduated from college. Your family is hosting a party in his honor. Your father has asked you to offer a two-minute speech in praise of your brother. Draft an outline.

23. Attend to disposition and delivery
Use prudence to judge your disposition.
Avoid tics. Check the chairs. Arrive early.

23.1. Recall an occasion when you listened to a speaker who came with a poor disposition. What made it defective?

23.2. Draft a one-minute chat on the topic "My favorite author these days." Deliver it before a friend. What tics did they notice? Observe them deliver the same.

24. Review intelligently
Record both the memorable and the forgettable.
"Anything worth doing is worth doing badly"
(G.K. Chesterton).

24.1. Prepare a list of questions you think would be helpful for your own review of a talk. Using this list, evaluate your one-minute chat on "My favorite author" (above, 23.2).

25. *Nihil nimius*
"The only difficulty was that though the universe had been disposed of, I myself was left over" (Walker Percy). Be more reliable than romantic. Make composition a habit. Nothing too much.

25.1. Reconstruct your current "method" of composition. Where do you do your intellectual work? At what hours? At what pace? With what results?

25.2. Consider examples of "romantics" and "reliables" whom you know. Describe the differences in their habits.

25.3. What are two practical steps you might take to conform your routine better to the counsel *nihil nimius*?

26. Wed truth to beauty
Beauty helps reconcile wisdom and power.

26.1. Name two deceased persons whom you admire for their ability to make truth appealing.

26.2 Name and describe someone living who combines wisdom and wit.

The Poems

First Poems to Memorize

Psalms 1, 23, and 100
Shakespeare, Sonnets 30, 116, and 146
George Herbert, "The Pulley"
John Donne, Holy Sonnet 14
Percy Shelley, "Love's Philosophy"
Wordsworth, "The World is Too Much With Us"
Newman, "Lead Kindly Light"
Hopkins, "God's Grandeur"
Frost, "Nothing Gold Can Stay"
Ogden Nash, "Word of Advice to Husbands"
Richard Wilbur, selections from "Opposites"

Further Poems...

Herbert, "Love"
Shelley, "Ozymandias"
Hopkins, "Pied Beauty"
G.K. Chesterton, "A Christmas Carol"
Dylan Thomas, "Do not go gentle into that good night"
Frost, "My November Guest"
Wilbur, "Teresa"
T.S. Eliot, opening to "The Wasteland"
Fulton Sheen, "Heaven is a City on a Hill"